contents

INTRODUCTION

Ready-made curtains and blinds can never be exactly the size and style you want, while made-to-measure throughout the home is prohibitively expensive, especially if you are hoping for some of the more luxurious co-ordinated or detailed effects. Yet with a little time and patience, and using only the most basic of sewing machines, you can achieve superb styling and a really professional finish in return for very little skill and effort – and for a fraction of the cost. Even if you have never made your own curtains or blinds before, the basic techniques are very simple – much more so than dressmaking skills, for example – and once you have mastered these you can move on easily to more elaborate and creative effects.

The only real effort involved lies in taking strictly accurate measurements, and in matching up any pattern on the fabric if you are not using a plain or small all-over design, but the benefits in producing wholly individual and often imaginative results far outweigh the time and trouble involved in paying this attention to detail. To begin with, you can choose exactly the fabric you want to co-ordinate or contrast with other furnishings, maybe even selecting something other than conventional furnishing fabric such as muslin, coloured felt or inexpensive sheeting, on to which you have hand painted or stencilled your own designs using fabric paints. Then, you might choose to have one large curtain swept to the side instead of two conventional smaller ones. Instead of a plain lined curtain you could add a coloured lining, decorative trims or an elaborate heading. You could then expand your ideas with matching or co-ordinated effects combining several treatments: a blind and curtains in the same fabric, perhaps; an ornate pelmet to transform the window into a real showcase; or home-made accessories such as tie-backs and curtain pulls, cushions, tablecloths and lampshades all made from left-over fabric.

Windows are such an important focal point in most rooms that the success of the overall decorative scheme can depend on their treatment. Individual attention will immediately give them special impact and provide the inspiration for the rest of the soft furnishings. You can use blinds or curtains to give a fine window greater prominence or, equally, to blend a less interesting one almost out of existence, according to the demands of your design plans. You will find many clever design ideas and visual tricks that can be played with window treatments on pages 88–93.

By designing and dressing your own windows, you can gear them exactly to your practical needs, too. Linings and interlinings can be used not only to screen out light and noise, but also to provide excellent insulation against heat loss in winter. They help a curtain to hang well too, instantly making an inexpensive fabric look more luxurious. Sometimes the position of a window makes conventional curtain treatments unworkable – where there is not enough room to pull them back, for example, or where the window is an unusual or awkward shape or size. Here you can devise a specially shaped curtain, or one that lifts or drapes to suit its particular location. Blinds can be a more practical option in bathrooms, kitchens and children's rooms, where hanging curtains create a nuisance or even a hazard, but it can be difficult to find suitably stylish designs unless you make your own. From both a practical and an aesthetic point of view, then, making your own avoids having to 'make do' with a colour or design that is not-quite-right; or with slightly the wrong width or length, which will make even expensive ready-mades look substandard.

Having mastered the basic techniques, you will be able to go on to create other useful and attractive blind and curtain effects around the home. A thickly lined curtain hung from a stout pole can make all the difference to a draughty door. Blinds can be used as an inexpensive and practical alternative to cupboard doors to screen off shelves, or as a more stylish option to doors in a between-rooms serving hatch. You might fit shirred curtains, in a fabric to match other furnishings, to screen the glass in cupboard doors. Making your own shower curtains offers the chance to use more creative and exciting designs than are generally available in the ready-made market – the list goes on.

This book tells you everything you need to know in order to achieve any of these exciting and potentially stunning effects in your own home. In addition, the ideas you see here will hopefully inspire you to

Fitting fabric curtains behind glass doors can co-ordinate cupboards and cabinets with your window treatments.

try out many of your own creative designs on your windows, while the easy-to-follow, step-by-step instructions and practical pointers will help you achieve professional results every time, whether you are tackling the simplest curtain or a more elaborate co-ordinated effect. You will find chapters explaining exactly what tools and accessories you need in order to start work, the suitability of different fabrics for different effects, and what to look out for when you go shopping. Simple explanations take the mystery out of choosing between the various tracks and poles, show how different heading tapes produce a particular look and style, or present a foolproof way to measure up and calculate what you will need in the way of tools and materials for a specific project.

If you are looking for clever ways to transform a dull room, there are special sections on visual tricks and *trompe-l'oeil* effects that can be achieved simply by changing the size, shape and style of a particular window treatment. No-sew draped ideas and suggestions for cheaper fabrics prove that you do not have to spend a lot of money or be particularly handy with a needle to create an imaginative and stylish interior. Finally, the practical step-by-step projects take you gently through the stages required to complete a wide range of blind and curtain styles, from the simplest roller blind to a flounced festoon, or double frilled curtains complete with tie-backs and matching pelmet.

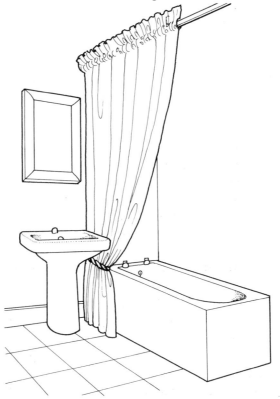

Making your own shower curtain can transform the bathroom.

With all the wonderful options available for different window treatments, it can be difficult to know where to start when choosing a style and fabric for your curtains and blinds. You will need to decide not only what will be suitable – indeed stunning – from a design point of view, while fitting in with the rest of your decor, but also what will be practical. You will pick up plenty of ideas and impressions from the projects in this book, as well as from photographs in other books and magazines. You may even have taken a special liking already to certain treatments and be keen to try them out in your own home. This enthusiasm will certainly make short work of the stitching involved, but do take care not to get too carried away and impose a style that might be unsuitable on a certain window or incongruous with the overall look of your home. The secret of success lies in keeping two determining factors at the back of your mind: firstly, the overall style and size of the room, and secondly, the shape, size and style of the window itself and how it will be used.

CONSIDER THE WINDOW

There are so many different sizes and styles of window, and some are definitely easier to dress than others. It can be very expensive to buy sufficient fabric for a large window, which may also be cold if curtains are not lined and interlined. Small windows, on the other hand, can present their own design problems when too cramped for conventional treatments. Newer properties might include large picture windows, where you do not want the treatment to dominate the room; older, cottage-style homes may lack the space even to erect traditional curtain poles or tracks.

Before you tackle problems such as these, there are practical points to consider as well. What restrictions does the window present by day, and by night? It may require free access for opening during the day, in which case a fixed treatment or one that cannot be swept back will be useless. At night, do you need to screen out unwelcome light or noise? How important is heat insulation? These considerations will influence not only the style of window dressing you choose, but also the fabric you use to create it. Does it need to be heavyweight, or would a light, gauzy effect suffice?

From a design point of view, the first important decision will be whether to play up the window or play it down within the general furnishing scheme of the room. You may well decide to make it a focal

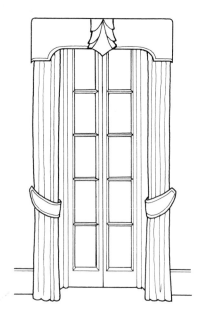

An elaborate pelmet and floor-length curtain can 'play up' a tall, narrow window, maximizing its impact.

point, especially if the window is particularly striking or attractive. In this case, it could form the starting point for other co-ordinated soft furnishings around the room, and may even dictate the style of the whole decorative scheme. Choose one of the grander or more eye-catching effects to set off or frame the window: a combination of treatments such as both blind and curtains, matching tie-backs or an ornate pelmet or valance will help give the window more prominence. Once you have selected the fabric, perhaps choosing a strong colour or bold pattern for extra impact, you could embellish the effect with a range of co-ordinated or contrasting accessories such as borders and braids, trims, tassels, tie-backs and pulls. For the rest of the room, paint and carpet colours could then be picked out from your curtain fabric, furniture upholstered in a matching fabric or one from the same range, and even the lighting could be arranged to highlight the window after dark.

Where you wish to play down the window and minimize its impact, perhaps to distract attention from a less-than-lovely view during the day, or to focus attention on another feature of the room such as a fine fireplace or some other object of architectural interest, take the opposite approach: use your existing furnishings and decorations to disguise the window and encourage it to blend into the background. If you design the rest of the room first, the window can be co-ordinated completely with surrounding wallpapers and fabrics by choosing matching materials. Select the simplest blind or curtain styles, hide an unpleasant view using pretty patterned nets, matching voiles or even a co-ordinated café curtain to cover the lower half of the window.

PROBLEM WINDOWS

Some windows present problems simply through their shape, size or position. A bay window, for example, precludes the use of decorative poles, but there are special curtain tracks available which curve easily around the length of the bay without impeding the movement of the curtains. Alternatively, a series of smaller curtains or individual blinds for each window usually works better than trying to accommodate larger effects.

French windows or modern sliding patio doors may also be difficult to dress successfully, both from a design and a practical point of view, especially where there is not sufficient room to sweep back a pair of curtains which may involve bulky fabrics and thick linings. A single curtain often does the job very well over a French window and can be held to one side stylishly using a tie-back, hook or wooden holdback (this is a useful way to treat any window which is tight to a corner or where there is a shortage of useful wall space). With a patio door you will be considering what is virtually wall-to-wall, floor-to-ceiling

A bay window can be dressed with several separate pairs of curtains.

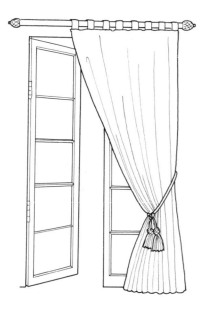

French windows demand floor-length curtains.

curtaining, and this vast areas of glass is probably best treated in this manner – as if you were designing a fabric wall. Modest pleating or shirring the fabric on to a narrow rail will draw less attention to the mass of fabric, and could always be continued around the corner if you need to pull the fabric right back during the day. The fabric itself could be matched to the wallpaper to complete the illusion.

Other windows that traditionally have presented design problems are the small circular or long narrow style often found in halls and on landings. These are frequently left without any kind of treatment at all, but can be dressed using a small pole or narrow brass rail – perhaps even a length of bamboo – on to which curtains can be threaded or hung to clear the window completely during the day. For circular and oddly shaped windows, a fixed curtain is sometimes the answer, made up to fit the size and shape of the window and fixed top and bottom on narrow rails to allow it to be pulled to one side. This treatment can also be adapted successfully to the sloping windows frequently seen in loft conversions and other roof lights. Both blinds and curtains can be fixed or fastened top and bottom to prevent them swinging outwards.

Older homes can present all kinds of knotty problems. Dormer windows are notoriously difficult to dress well: you can either fit a curtain inside the recess, where space is often too limited, or within the room, which might spoil the effect of the windows. Again, a pair of curtains or a single drape which can be pulled right back on an attractive rail to clear the window is often the most successful

Wall-to-wall shirred curtains are one way to handle large patio doors stylishly.

For deeply recessed cottage and dormer windows, curtains hung outside the recess may be more practical.

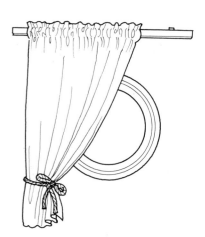

A small, single curtain may be the solution for an awkwardly sized or shaped window.

solution. Deep windowsills present a similar problem, although again, a rail within the room is frequently the best option. Remember, however, that plants and ornaments left marooned on the sill behind the curtains will be exposed to extreme temperatures at night.

You might also have old windows with attractively curved or arched lintels which you do not want to hide for fear of detracting from the character of the room. A wooden or brass pole is an attractive treatment that only partially disguises what lies behind; the alternative is to echo the shape with a rigid or fabric pelmet which at least avoids squaring it off and maintains that old-fashioned feel.

COLOUR, PATTERN AND DESIGN

The style of a particular window treatment will be dictated to a large extent by how you envisage the rest of the room. Roller and Roman blinds have a smart crispness that ideally suits a modern interior; flouncy festoons and curtains with plenty of fullness and additional accessories such as frills, pelmets and tie-backs naturally conjure up a more traditional atmosphere.

Once you have settled on a style, you will need to choose a suitable fabric. Firstly, should it be plain or patterned? Generally speaking plains are better if the room will be busy with a patterned carpet, upholstery or wallpaper. However, today's cleverly co-ordinated furnishing ranges make it easy to mix and match different papers and fabrics, combining large prints and tiny patterns with colour-matched stripes or even broken-colour effects, without creating too overpowering a scheme.

Texture

You will need to consider not just harmony within colour and pattern, but a good variety of textures as well. All shiny surfaces – with lots of polished wood, glazed cottons and other reflective finishes – would be very unrelaxing. Equally, too many thick velvets and other heavy fabrics at the windows, on the floor and covering the furniture would be stifling.

Purchasing Fabrics

The guidelines on page 20 describe many of the fabrics available, but you will still have to decide which type is best for the particular window treatment. Importantly, look only at the best-quality furnishing fabrics as these are strong, durable and resistant to fading. Dress fabric is not really suitable, being less hard wearing and available only in narrower widths, which means a lot of seams. Check that fabrics are fade and shrink resistant and can be washed or dry-cleaned easily, especially if they are for a heavy-wear areas such as the kitchen or living room. Ideally, take a look at how the fabric folds and hangs.

A deep pelmet above the window and floor-length curtains will make a window appear taller and narrower.

This will also give you an opportunity to see how any pattern on the fabric appears once it is hung in folds. If you really cannot visualize how it will look, it is well worth buying a small piece and pinning it up in the right position: it is interesting how different patterns and colour can appear when viewed from various points within a room, or with the light behind rather than directly on them. You can also experiment with the effect a lining will have on the fabric, and compare it with other furnishings in the room for compatibility.

VISUAL TRICKS

Even when you have settled the question of style, colour and finish, and whether or not you want linings, trimmings, pelmets and other practical and decorative accessories, there is still the question of length and width to consider. This is crucial not just to the overall look of the window, but also for ordering the correct amount of fabric and the right size pole or track. By adjusting these dimensions you can also play visual tricks with your window, making it appear much larger or smaller than it really is according to how prominent it is to be in the room.

Extending the rail or pole well beyond the window area will create an impression of extra width, while a wide pelmet heading a floor-length drop of curtains will make the window seem elegantly tall. The simple addition of a few extra metres (yards) of fabric can transform a dull or hitherto unimportant window into a real focal point. Even where space is limited you can experiment with blinds and dress curtains, where curtains are permanently gathered to the sides for ornamental effect only – a wonderfully economical option when you cannot afford a lot of fabric. To create the opposite effect a ruched or

Extending the curtain rail or pole beyond the window will give an impression of width.

Sill-length curtains or tie-backs, as here, are the answer where there is a radiator or piece of furniture under the window.

flounced blind, or even a Roman blind for a less fussy look, used in conjunction with matching curtains will visually reduce a window in size, especially if you fasten the curtains together in the centre and sweep them back on either side. Use a large bow, rosette or similar decoration to highlight the effect where the curtains meet.

Generally speaking, curtains should fall either to sill or floor – never somewhere in between. Remember that floor-length curtains are most costly and pick up dirt more easily, but can be warmer provided they are not concealing a radiator. Blinds are almost always sill-length, but can be fitted within the window recess or beyond it depending on the effect you want to achieve.

ROOM BY ROOM

Each room will have its own specific requirements, and these too should be considered when choosing the ideal window treatment. The **living room** will give curtains (or blinds) hard wear, but the overall effect needs to be luxurious, even sumptuous, depending on your general taste and style. Even the simplest, most understated effects should have that stamp of quality and a professional finish to look comfortable here. This is where the choice of quality fabrics, linings and interlinings and attention to small details really pay off. You may also have to co-ordinate your window treatment with other furnishings and, on a practical level, decide how well insulated the windows need to be for comfort.

In the **dining room** overall style and use will dictate the window treatment: grand drapes to make a regal setting for traditional dinners enjoyed by flickering candlelight and the sparkle of crystal; perhaps just a cheery roller blind where its purpose is primarily that of a sunny breakfast room; while the country-cottage owner seeking a little privacy might opt for frilled café curtains along the lower half of the window.

In the **kitchen**, practical demands must be considered before style: curtains may not be a good choice, especially near the cooking area where they might become a fire hazard, and blinds are a more popular option. Choose a bright roller blind – or even a jolly picture to enliven washing-up sessions – while for a softer, more feminine look in a less utilitarian kitchen you might select one of the flouncier blind options. Blinds or curtains, it is essential that the fabric is easy to clean.

Similarly, **bathroom** windows can be difficult to handle successfully. The fabric used must be able to withstand extremes of temperature, steam, powder and wet hands without becoming limp and tired, and the windows themselves are often small or awkwardly placed. Again, an easy-wipe roller blind is a practical and popular option, but if you prefer to soften the look, especially against a background of hard, shiny tiles and clinical-looking sanitaryware, this might be combined with a pair of pretty dress curtains held out of the

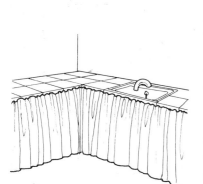

Curtains can be an attractive alternative to cupboard doors in the kitchen, but keep them away from the cooking area.

way with matching tie-backs.

Bedrooms might demand a wide variety of treatments depending on your personal style and practical requirements. Many people prefer light, unlined curtains with a simple heading so that the morning sunshine can stream in. Others demand thick linings to screen out maximum light and noise at night: certainly a heavier fabric and good lining will create a cosier, more luxurious look if you are trying to provide a more traditional atmosphere. For the feminine touch, the addition of a frilled pelmet and flounced blind can be co-ordinated with other frilly touches around the room. Alternatively, go for a more masculine or understated atmosphere by doing away with curtains and choosing a smart Roman blind, provided it offers sufficient insulation against light and cold.

In **children's rooms**, practical needs must again be put first: the windows must be safe (long curtains are out), fabrics must be easy to keep clean, and the room must be warm and free from draughts. It is also helpful if curtains or blinds are thick enough to cut down light and noise during the day as well as at night while children are still young enough to be taking daytime naps. A thick roller blind is an obvious choice and can be decorated in bright primary colours or with the children's favourite nursery characters. However, curtains have the advantage that they can be thickly lined and easily removed for cleaning. The best solution is probably blind and curtains, which gives you flexibility and almost total black-out when both are drawn.

FINISHING TOUCHES

There are many decorative finishing touches that can be applied to blinds, curtains, pelmets and tie-backs to personalize them and make them that little bit special. Many are easily made from scraps of left-over fabric, or a wide range of suitable trims can be bought from the haberdashery department of furnishing specialists. If you cannot find exactly the colour you need, then dye it: some stores offer a dyeing service.

A decorative edging will often give curtains or blinds that extra touch of interest and impact. Choose from frills, lace or broderie Anglaise or, for a less fussy, feminine look, braid, tassels or tiny pompons – perhaps even a contrasting binding. Extra decorations – fabric rosettes, bows, appliqué, ribbons, even coloured buttons – can be stitched or glued in an eyecatching central position or anywhere on curtains, pelmets and tie-backs.

If you do not want to make fabric tie-backs but your curtains need fastening to the side, a wide range of ready-made holdbacks is available, from thick tasselled cords to be fastened around chunky cleats or hooks, to wooden mushrooms and brass scrolls, and even novelty shapes like hands, animals and flowers. Other useful curtain

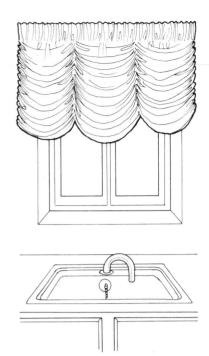

An Austrian blind is both pretty and practical in the kitchen.

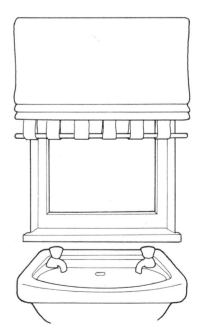

A Roman blind is smart for bathrooms and does not get in the way.

accessories you might like to consider include wooden pulls and pulley systems that enable you to pull curtains without touching the fabric and make it grubby; and wooden acorns and tassel pulls for fastening to blinds. You can even fit electronically controlled curtains to be drawn by remote control from the comfort of your armchair! This device can be connected to a time-controlled switch which enables the curtains to be pulled and drawn back even while you are away, as a deterrent to burglars.

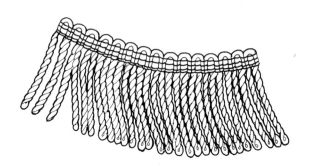

Fringed trimming for curtains, pelmets and blinds.

If you have not done a lot of sewing, before you start work you will need to review the tools and accessories required for actually putting together your curtains or blinds. It also helps to familiarize yourself with the different types of fabric available before you buy. The width of fabric, its weight, finish and even its pattern will affect the way any item is constructed, and can influence the hang and appearance of the finished curtains. You will also need to understand the differences between the various styles of heading tape or blind components.

THE SEWING BOX
You may already have some sewing essentials at home. Check that pins and needles are not rusty or they will mark your fabric, and make a list of anything which is missing or needs replacing.

Scissors
Always buy best-quality scissors and proper fabric shears for cutting out, and do not allow them to be used for anything else. It also pays to keep them well sharpened.

You will need a pair of 20–23cm (8–9in) cutting-out shears and a small pair of sharp scissors for snipping threads, seams and other odd jobs. A pair of pinking shears which produces a zig-zag ('pinked') edge to trimmed fabric can be useful as a quick alternative to prevent fabric fraying.

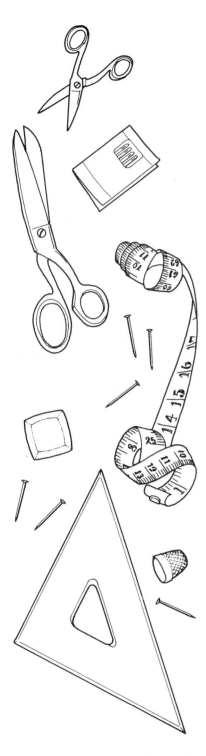

Needles

You will need a variety of needles – those labelled 'sharps' and 'betweens' are the most useful – in different sizes for stitching with various threads and fabrics.

Pins

Buy a box of quality steel dressmaking pins: they will last longer and give better service. Some kind of pincushion is useful when using and removing pins and prevents too many getting lost; you can easily make up one yourself by covering a large, smooth stone or similar weighty object with padding and fabric. This can also be useful for holding down fabric when stitching curtains and blinds.

Thimble

A thimble is not such an old-fashioned idea when pushing a sharp-ended needle through thick layers of fabric. To save frayed fingers, buy the metal sort, as plastic splits too easily.

Tailor's Chalk

Never use a pencil or pen for marking furnishing fabrics as it can be difficult, if not impossible, to remove and on some fabrics may damage the pile. Special tailor's chalk is available in a variety of colours: white is the easiest to rub off, but you may need one other colour for pale fabrics and when making a variety of marks.

Tape Measure

A fibreglass or linen dressmaker's tape measure is useful. If yours is an old one check it carefully, as they tend to stretch over time. Even more useful is a rigid rule or metre (yard) stick for marking an accurate straight line. Made from plastic, metal or wood, these are available from decorating and art shops.

Set Square

A large set square is very useful for getting an accurate right-angle when cutting out fabric.

SEWING MACHINES

If you are a quick, neat – and patient – hand sewer, there is no real reason why you should not make up all your own home furnishings by hand. However, those long seams can be laborious, especially if there are many widths of fabric to join, and even the simplest sewing machine makes quick work of these basic sewing requirements. Provided you are not intending to do any fancy stitching, basic reconditioned machines can be purchased quite cheaply second-hand, although the option of a zig-zag facility for neatening edges and seams

Equip yourself with a well-stocked sewing box.

is useful if you can get it. You might even consider it worth investing in a brand-new machine with a wide range of stitch options including hemming, buttonholing and even embroidery. Do shop around, as even major brand names are available at competitive prices from discount stores. If you are planning to do a lot of sewing, an electrically powered machine can be quicker and operates via a foot pedal which leaves the hands free to manoeuvre the fabric more easily and accurately.

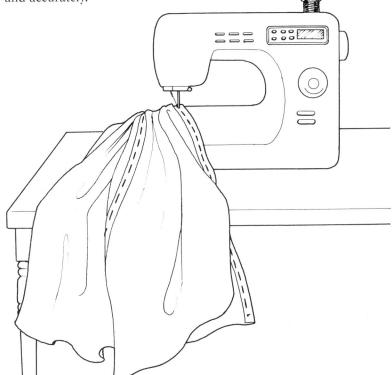

Many modern sewing machines can offer a wide range of computerized stitches, but the very basic machines are adequate for simple curtain-making techniques.

OTHER ESSENTIAL EQUIPMENT

You will need a large, flat surface for cutting out; if you do not have a suitable table or work surface at home, a clean wallpapering table makes a practical alternative. You will also require an iron and ironing board for pressing seams and fabric at every stage of construction (see page 27).

FABRICS

It is not just colour and pattern that will influence the final appearance of your blinds and curtains: the *type* of fabric you choose will make a big difference too, not just visually but also from a practical point of view. Thicker, weightier fabrics like velvet and linen have good insulation properties and a much richer, more expensive feel which is ideally suited to traditional-style living or dining rooms, but might look out of place in a bedroom or bathroom. Lighter, flimsier fabrics require lining and plenty of width to hang well. They look young and fresh in the right setting, but teamed with the wrong furnishings can give the impression that you have had to skimp on costs. Fabric is often available in a choice of weights and types for a variety of co-ordinated furnishing effects. Fabric for blinds will need to be chosen particularly carefully, as anything too thick and bulky will not gather or roll correctly. Remember too that the weight and style of the curtain fabric will affect your choice of pole or track (see pages 84–87) as some of the cheaper, smaller types will not be man enough for the job.

Types of Fabric

Fabrics are made from either manmade or natural fibres. This affects their feel, wear and care. Manmade fibres are often manufactured from chemically treated raw materials, such as vegetables, which gives them a natural look or feel but means they can only be washed or cleaned according to strict instructions. Natural fibres include silk, wool, cotton or linen and in recent years these have increasingly been mixed with manmade fibres to reduce cost and improve their wearing qualities. Always be fully aware of what you are buying and how it will perform; it may help to keep a note of the washing or dry-cleaning instructions for future reference – nothing is worse, when you have taken the time and trouble to make them yourself, than being faced with a pair of shrunk curtains.

Synthetics include the ubiquitous and popular **polyester** which is strong and crease resistant, does not fade easily in sunlight and resists dirt and dust. It washes easily without shrinking. **Nylon** is hardwearing, dirt resistant and creaseproof, but does fade in strong sunlight. **Acrylics** are more stable and will not fade, shrink or stretch. **Acetate** has good insulating properties and is durable and dirt resistant, but can be weakened by washing and strong sunlight. All three melt rather than burn at high temperatures. **Rayon viscose** is another synthetic that is usually blended with other fabrics to improve its resistance to sunlight and creasing.

Cotton is one of the most popular natural fabrics: it is hardwearing and takes printing and dyeing well. Different finishes are available to improve its shrink, crease, fade and water resistance. Even stronger, and an excellent heavy-weight natural furnishing fabric, is **linen**. This has good dirt resistance and will not shrink. Because it creases easily, linen is frequently mixed with other fibres such as cotton or polyester. **Silk** is a natural but expensive fabric with a distinctive sheeny finish. Although it is strong and durable (and dyes well, so is available in a wide range of beautiful colours), it will fade if exposed to strong sunlight. **Wool** is particularly durable and also dyes well. It can be treated to ensure shrink resistance but is more often blended with synthetic fibres to create a strong, crease-resistant fabric.

Fabric Names

Knowledge of a few traditional names may help when choosing and buying furnishing fabrics.

Baize
Lightweight woollen felt, traditionally dyed green and used for covering billiard tables but can be used for roller blinds.

Brise-bise
Plain or sometimes patterned lace or net curtain hung across the lower half of a window.

Brocade
Silk or satin-based luxury fabric with a jacquard (elaborately figured) pattern.

Broderie Anglaise
Lightly woven cotton featuring an embroidered effect of small holes.

Buckram
Coarse, plain-weave cotton fabric stiffened for use as linings and, if heavyweight, for making pelmets.

Bump
Cotton wadding used as an interlining to give weight and warmth to curtains.

Calico
Plain woven fabric heavier than muslin, which can be bleached or natural.

Canvas
Strong cloth made from cotton, polyester or nylon and in a choice of weights and qualities, suitable for roller blinds.

Crêpe
Knitted or woven fabric with a puckered appearance.

Crushed velvet
Velvet fabric with a permanently flattened pile, producing an irregular finish.

Damask
Jacquard-woven, figured fabric which uses the contrast between the satin and sateen areas of the design to make a pattern.

Dimity
Cotton fabric with checks or stripes woven into it.

Domette
Plain cloth made of cotton and wool.

Dupion
Irregular slub silk fabric, or imitation of that effect.

Felt
Soft fabric with a matt, non-woven appearance, usually made from wool or a wool mixture of fibres.

Flannelette
Thick, soft, heavy cotton with a raised nap, traditionally used for winter bedsheets but an economical alternative for interlining curtains.

Gingham
Light cotton fabric with a regular checked pattern in green, red, blue, yellow or black, all on white.

Hessian
Coarse, loosely woven fabric made from jute or hemp fibres.

Holland
Glazed, medium-weight fabric in plain cotton or linen, traditionally used for window blinds.

Hopsack
Basketweave-effect fabric.

Jacquard
Highly figured and multi-coloured effect produced by the Jacquard loom.

Lawn
Sheer, lightweight fabric with a soft, smooth, plain-woven finish made from cotton, linen or polyester.

Muslin
Fine, lightweight fabric with a plain, open weave.

Net
Open-meshed sheer fabric.

Organdie
Lightweight but strong fabric, like muslin but with a stiff, colourless finish.

Percale
Quality cotton cloth with a close, plain weave, usually used as superior bedsheeting fabric.

Sateen
Fabric with a smooth, lustrous surface often used for curtain linings.

Satin
Sheeny fabric similar to sateen.

Seersucker
Fabric with a puckered pattern, usually sporting stripes or checks.

Shantung
Plain-woven fabric made from wild silk.

Slub
Fabric usually made from wild silk, linen or certain synthetic fibres which has short, thickened bars appearing randomly along its length.

Toile de Jouy
Printed cotton imitating a traditional eighteenth-century French style, which featured finely detailed engraved scenes in a single colour.

Union
Mixed-fibre fabric with one type of fibre running in the warp yarn and another in the weft, such as linen/cotton or cotton/wool.

Velvet
Thick, luxurious-looking fabric with a short-cut pile and a brushed finish.

Voile
Lightweight, open-textured fabric, stiffer than muslin and often used to screen windows, in the same way as nets.

Lining Fabrics

If you choose to line or interline your curtains, or certain styles of window blind, you will have to buy a suitable fabric that will complement the main fabric and help it to hang well. The linings can be hung separately – there are facilities for this on most styles of curtain rail – which is a useful option where the curtains are removed frequently for washing or are changed for a lighter-weight fabric in summer. However, detachable linings do not hang as well as those that are sewn in.

Cotton sateen is commonly used for linings: it is closely woven and available in a wide range of colours, although white and natural are frequently used. Do not try to tear this fabric as it will rip unevenly: cut cleanly with sharp fabric shears. You can also buy an aluminium-coated lining material which has good insulating properties and is useful where you wish to reduce noise or light. It pays to buy the better-quality lining fabrics as these are less likely to shrink when washed or dry cleaned.

Interlining for curtains improves the way they hang and gives them a thick, luxurious look as well as increasing their insulating properties, keeping in the heat and cutting out more light and noise from outside. A loosely woven, soft fabric such as bump or even flannelette sheeting can be used for interlining.

SEWING THREAD

Buy sufficient thread at the same time as you purchase the fabric for your blinds or curtains, so that you can choose the correct shade. The thread should be a slightly darker colour than that of the fabric; if you are using a multi-coloured design, pick out the predominant shade. Synthetic threads are for use with manmade fibres, while cotton or cotton-coated polyester threads should be chosen for stitching natural fibres.

The threads are marked in a choice of sizes: No 40 is for sewing heavyweight fabrics, No 50 is for medium and lightweight fabrics, as well as silk, and No 60 is for the finest materials. A large reel of inexpensive black or white basting cotton for tacking is essential if you do not want to waste your more expensive coloured threads.

HEADING TAPES

Your choice of heading tape will directly influence the finished effect of the curtains, and will also dictate the total amount of fabric you will need and number of widths required for each curtain. When planning one of the fuller, more elaborate types make sure that you can actually afford the amount of fabric required: sometimes it is better to choose a cheaper fabric to achieve that sumptuous fullness, using linings or interlinings to add body and richness, than to spoil an expensive fabric with an inappropriate heading. Buy only the better-quality heading tapes, as nothing is more irritating then cheap cords snapping when you pull them to gather up your completed curtain.

Simple Gathers

These use the standard narrow heading tape and will require one and a half times the width of your track. This simple effect is often enough for unlined bedroom curtains or where the heading will be concealed behind a pelmet or gathered valance.

Pencil Pleats

These produce a more elaborate, deeper-pleated effect, created by using a special, wider heading tape that gathers the fabric into crisp folds. This heading requires two and a half times the width of the track.

Pinch Pleats

Traditionally, these were painstakingly marked and hand stitched, but today you can buy a special drawstring tape which gathers the fabric into a series of regularly spaced double pleats, which look particularly good hung from a decorative pole. This heading requires two and a half to three times the width of the pole or track.

Standard heading tape.

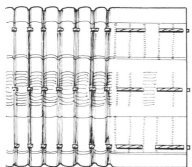

Pencil-pleating tape.

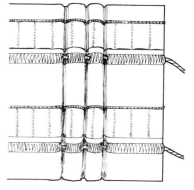

Regularly spaced pinch pleats on a special drawstring tape.

Box Pleats

This is a very professional-looking, hand-stitched effect which uses three times the width of the track and gathers the fabric into wide pleats at approximately 30cm (12in) intervals. Importantly, the total width of each curtain needs to be divisible by 30cm (12in).

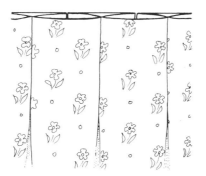

Wide, hand-stitched box pleats.

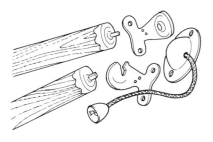

Roller blind kit.

Blinds

Special tapes, cords and battens are also available for creating the specific effects of Austrian and Roman blinds. You can buy kits for roller blinds which include a spring-mechanism roller, stiffening solution for applying to your fabric, battens, cords and even a pull; alternatively, these components can be bought separately.

Hooks

You will also require a selection of small, usually plastic but sometimes metal, hooks to attach the heading to the track. It is not a good idea to skimp on hooks, as the curtain will not hang correctly and may even droop or come down. The most common type of hook has a double bend with a small extra bend to hold it in place. You can also buy special hooks which feature long prongs and are designed to fit into the heading tape used for creating pinch pleats. Brass-pronged hooks are available for hand-gathered headings.

WEIGHTS

As an additional aid to help quality lined curtains hang well, special weights can be used in the hem. These can be purchased loose for sewing into the corners of the hems when they are mitred, or in chains or strips for slotting through the hem when it is taken up. Traditionally, coins were used and owners of old houses sometimes dream of finding a fortune in gold sovereigns hidden in the hems of their old curtains!

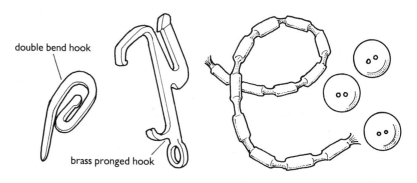

double bend hook

brass pronged hook

Curtain hooks for hand-pleated and tape headings.

Single curtain weights for corners and a string of weights for slotting through curtain hems.

Once you have decided on and designed the window effect you want and have chosen the fabric, you can use that information to measure up and calculate exactly what materials you need. You *must* have these details to hand when you venture out to buy heading tapes, fabrics and trims: accurate measurements are absolutely essential for success in creating your own window treatments. Too little fabric will result in a skimped look; too much is a waste of money unless you can use it to make up matching cushions, tie-backs or other co-ordinated soft furnishings.

MEASURING UP

When measuring up for curtains, the pole or track must be in place so that you get the width and length just right. Curtains should reach to just below the window or to the floor – never somewhere in between, which just looks as though you ran out of fabric or could not make up your mind where to finish them. You will also need to know how much fabric your chosen curtain heading will require: one and a half times the width for a simple gathered heading; two and a half times the width for pencil pleats; two and a half to three times the width for pinch pleats; and three times for box pleats. The more sophisticated, hand-finished effects like box and pinch pleats need to be calculated absolutely accurately across the width so that you do not end up with half a pleat at the end of the line.

Measuring up for curtains.

Calculating Width

When calculating fabric for blinds, measure just inside or outside the window frame. The type of blind – a simple, stiffened roller blind or one of the ruched and pleated effects – will determine whether you need to allow extra width for a small hem or for gathering tapes.

Curtain widths must take into consideration whether you are going to cover the window with a pair of curtains, with one large curtain swept to the side or, where the window is a large one, with several separate curtains. To work out how much fabric is required for a pair of curtains, divide the necessary width by two, allowing for an overlap in the centre by adding 10–15cm (4–6in) to each curtain width. A further 6cm (2½in) will be required on each side for hems. The sum total will give you the flat width required for each curtain.

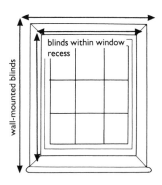

Measuring up for blinds.

Now calculate how many of these widths are required to accommodate your chosen heading. Divide this figure by the width of your fabric to calculate how many fabric widths will be required. Add a further 1.5cm (½in) for seams at each width join. If you have to use a half or an odd number of widths, try to use complete panel widths in the centre of each curtain, with the cut widths put to the sides to create a professional and balanced appearance. The width (and length) of linings and interlinings will need to be the same as that of the main curtain fabric, with perhaps a slightly smaller allowance for hems.

Calculating Length

When you have measured from pole or track to sill or floor, add 15cm (6in) for each hem and 7.5cm (3in) for the headings. In older properties it is a good idea to double check that your pole or track is straight by using a spirit level; measure the curtain length on both sides to make sure that there is no discrepancy due to sloping walls or ceilings.

Pattern Matching

Patterned fabric requires extra fabric to allow for pattern matching, and this will depend on the size and scale of the particular design you have chosen.

Calculate how many complete pattern widths will be needed for each curtain length, starting at the top of the curtain for floor-length curtains and at the lower hem for sill-length ones. Where two or more fabric widths are required across the curtain, the pattern must be correctly matched at each join by pressing and pinning the two pieces together so that they achieve an exact match. You will need to allow for wastage when calculating how much fabric to buy.

When purchasing your fabric, check that there are no marks, flaws or pulled threads on the piece you are taking home. As with wallpaper, you should buy your fabric from one roll only, as colour dyes can vary. In addition, patterns are not always printed accurately in relation to the straight grain of the fabric and this can create a lopsided look to the finished curtains. To check whether the pattern is straight, fold back a small piece of the fabric, wrong sides together, selvedge to selvedge, and check whether the pattern runs correctly along the fold. If the difference is noticeable, select another fabric.

CUTTING OUT

Make sure you have all the necessary heading tapes, thread and lining fabrics to hand before you start cutting out. Remember, once the fabric is cut mistakes cannot be rectified, so make sure that the fabric is laid out correctly and that you double-check your calculations.

You will need a clean, flat surface on which to work; if you do not have a large square or rectangular table, a scrubbed wallpaper trestle – or even the floor, if it is clean and level – may make a practical

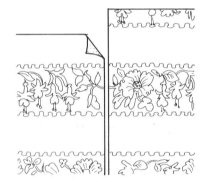

Head curtains with the same pattern repeat.

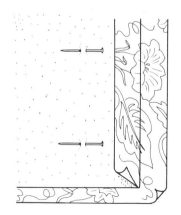

Pattern matching for fabric joins.

alternative. Cut cleanly and keep widths cut completely straight. Never use the pattern as a guide, as the fabric will often stretch or move out of line: use a set square at right-angles to the selvedge to ensure a straight cut. In some fabrics you can draw a thread to achieve a straight line across the grain.

When you have measured the length of the first width of fabric, remembering to take into account hems and headings, mark it with pins using a rigid ruler and then draw along the line with tailor's chalk and cut. Cut out the other lengths in the same way, taking care to allow for pattern matching and marking the top of each length with tailor's chalk to ensure that you hang them all the same way – this is important with pile fabrics such as velvet. Fit and pin together widths for joining as appropriate, and lay lengths together ready for stitching.

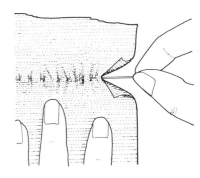

Drawing a thread will provide an accurate cutting line on some fabrics.

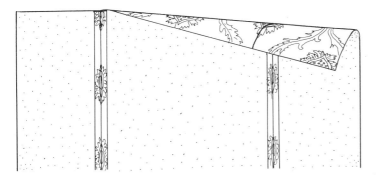

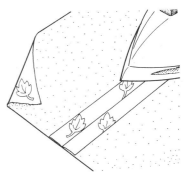

Use half-widths to centralize a large design when joining fabric widths.

PRESSING

When making up blinds and curtains, the fabric should be well pressed at every stage. This not only prevents the fabric becoming over-creased, but also ensures a neat finish to hems and seams. Remove any pins or tacking threads before pressing as these can mark the fabric. Test the temperature of the iron first on a piece of scrap fabric, gradually increasing the heat from the lowest setting. Velvets and some synthetic fabrics cannot be ironed, although seams can be steam pressed from the reverse if you are careful not to crush the pile. Always make sure that your iron is kept clean by rubbing the surface with a proprietary cleaner when it is turned off.

Pressing seams open ensures a flat finish.

SEWING GUIDE

If you have not done a lot of sewing before, you will need to familiarize yourself with the various sewing techniques used in making soft furnishings. There are various ways of stitching a seam, for example, depending on the type of fabric and the effect you want to achieve. Whenever you are joining two pieces of fabric or are applying a lining or trim, whether you are stitching by hand or using a sewing machine, there are two main aims: strength and permanence, and a neat, preferably invisible finish.

Seams

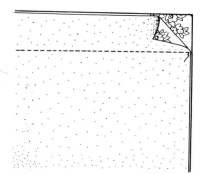 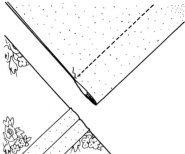 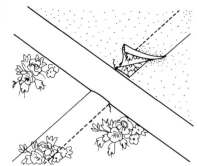

1 The most commonly used seam technique in making blinds and curtains is a **flat seam**. Place the raw edges of two pieces of fabric together, right sides facing, and stitch approximately 13mm (½in) from the edge. Where the edges might fray, neaten them using a zig-zag machine stitch or overcasting by hand (see page 30).

2 Where the raw edges need to be enclosed – on unlined curtains for example – you may prefer to use a **French seam**. This is only suitable for lighter-weight fabrics as it is quite bulky. Place the raw edges together, wrong sides facing, and stitch approximately 13mm (½in) from the edge. Trim the seams close to the stitching line to ensure that they lie as flat as possible, then place the fabric right sides together and machine stitch along the new seam line.

3 A **flat fell seam** is another method of making a strong seam which encloses the raw edges but leaves the stitching visible on the right side of the fabric. Place the raw edges of the fabric together, wrong sides facing, and stitch about 13mm (½in) from the edge. Trim only one side of the seam to 6mm (¼in) and turn a 3mm (⅛in) hem on the other side and fold over onto the trimmed seam. Stitch the fold into place along the right side of the fabric.

Temporary Stitching

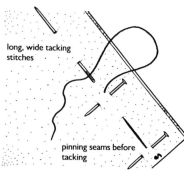

long, wide tacking stitches

pinning seams before tacking

Pieces of fabric may simply be pinned together to ensure that they are in the right position, but this is not ideal for stitching seams as the pins tend to get in the way. For good straight stitching and a professional finish, it is best to tack the fabric together and then remove the pins.

1 **Tacking** is simply the application of large, temporary stitches secured with a backstitch, so that they can be removed easily once the piece has been properly stitched. The tacking stitches are kept loose and are worked from right to left.

2 **Slip tacking** is used specificially for joining fabric widths where a pattern repeat needs matching. You can achieve an accurate match by first pinning the two pieces of fabric together as if making a plain seam, but ensuring a perfect pattern match. With right side facing, take a loose stitch through the fold on one side and into the single layer of fabric on the other. This should hold it exactly in place while you machine stitch the join.

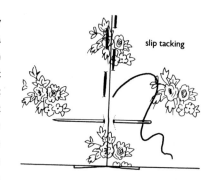

slip tacking

Hand Stitching

There is a range of useful hand-stitched effects for situations where it is not practicable to use the sewing machine, or where you want to achieve an invisible finish.

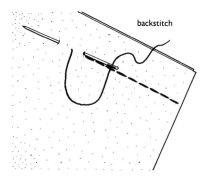

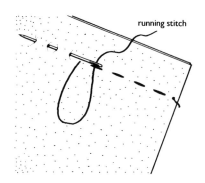

1 In **backstitch** the needle is worked from right to left to create a continuous series of strong, even stitches around 6mm (¼in) long. It involves taking the needle backwards the length of the stitch and bringing it out forwards ready for the next stitch.

2 **Running stitch** is not so strong and is used mainly for gathering fabric. Small, equal stitches are simply worked from right to left.

Other, more loosely applied stitches are used specifically for finishing off or holding fabric in position.

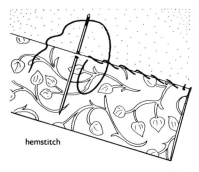

hemstitch

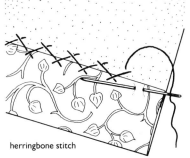

herringbone stitch

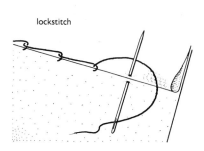

lockstitch

3 **Hemstitch** is essential for a smart finish and relies on neat stitching and the thread not being pulled too tightly. Working from right to left, on the wrong side of the fabric, the stitches pick up a mere thread of fabric just under the fold of the hem.

4 To secure the hems on interlined curtains, **herringbone stitch** is recommended. This creates a criss-cross effect over the raw edge and is worked from left to right.

5 **Lockstitch** is an even longer, looser stitch which is used mainly to hold curtain linings and interlinings in position. Working from left to right, the stitches run down the length of the curtain.

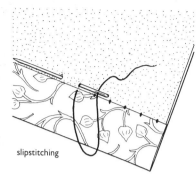

slipstitching

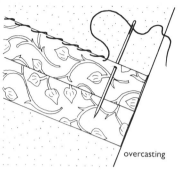

overcasting

6 **Slipstitch** can also be used to hold curtain linings in position. Here the needle picks up a thread on each fold of the two sides of fabric and is run about 6mm (¼in) along inside the fold before making the next stitch. Again, it is important not to pull the thread too tightly.

7 Lastly, there are stitches intended to neaten raw edges and prevent fraying. If your sewing machine does not have a zig-zag facility, then edges can be **overcast**: simply take the thread over and over the raw edge, taking care not to pull too tightly.

Mitring Corners

A mitred corner is a neat and professional-looking way to finish off the corners of curtains and tie-backs.

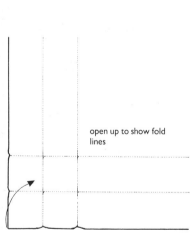

open up to show fold lines

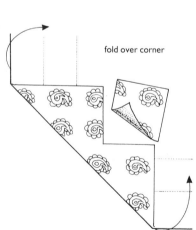

fold over corner

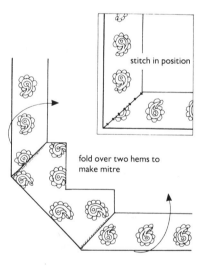

stitch in position

fold over two hems to make mitre

1 First press the hems in position, then open out the fabric again to show the fold marks.

2 Fold over the corner of the fabric at right angles to follow the line of the marks: it may be necessary to trim away some of the fabric to reduce the bulk if it is thick.

3 Fold the two edges of the hem according to the press lines and slipstitch the corner into place.

the projects

The individual projects that follow will take you easily through the techniques required to create a wide range of exciting window treatments. Although none are really difficult – even for a novice home-furnisher – you will find that this section starts with the most basic steps for making your own simple blinds and curtains, and progresses to more elaborate styles and interesting variations. Finally, you will find instructions for tackling those special finishing touches that are so important for achieving a really professional look.

unlined dress curtains

This quick and easy project could be used to make up any kind of basic unlined curtains: the only distinction of dress curtains is that they are purely ornamental, and your fabric will be calculated not to cover the whole window but to give a reasonable semblance of folds and pleats at either side (opposite). Unlined curtains may not offer much in the way of insulation in winter, but they have a lovely light, airy effect – especially if made up in a lightweight fabric – which is very attractive for summer curtains and in bedrooms. If pulled during daylight, they provide a pleasant filtered effect rather than total blackout, which may be desirable in some rooms.
Unlined curtains do not have much body so do not hang as well as lined and interlined curtains, and they are not really suited to the more elaborate heading effects.

Above: For a light and airy breakfast room, a fresh floral in pretty pastels is
the perfect complement to the clean lines of stripped timber and shiny
chrome.

CURTAIN FABRIC
MATCHING THREAD
PINS AND/OR TACKING THREAD
HEADING TAPE
CURTAIN RAIL
WEIGHTS (OPTIONAL)

This is the most basic curtain-making technique and it requires very little sewing skill to achieve professional results. The measuring up is important, however, so make sure you double-check your calculations before you start cutting the fabric. You must also ensure that the material is completely straight before cutting and stitching and that you line up any pattern.

When you have mastered the simple technique of unlined curtains, you may be inspired to make them for areas of the home other than windows. Curtains can be a great decorative device for those on a budget looking for a little instant impact or clever camouflage. For example, use curtains instead of doors on units in the kitchen, or to disguise pipework beneath a basin in the bathroom. A small floral print, fresh gingham or smart stripes would capture the traditional country effect of curtains used in this way.

For a more sophisticated effect, insert curtains behind the glass of cupboards and cabinets in the bathroom, kitchen or bedroom. This effect means that you can co-ordinate cupboards and units with furnishings and accessories in the room.

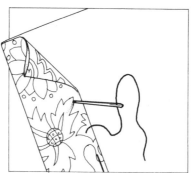

1 Estimate the amount of fabric you need for dress curtains by measuring the width you want to cover and allowing double. Make up the width for each curtain by joining fabric widths where necessary, using a flat seam and taking care to match any pattern. Snip the selvedges at 5cm (2in) intervals to prevent puckering. Press seams open.

2 Taking each new continuous width of fabric as your curtain, turn over 3cm (1¼in) on each long side and make this into a double hem, by folding the fabric over twice, ensuring that you keep the fold straight and even. Press flat and tack into position, then hemstitch the hem into place by hand as neatly as possible. Remove the tacking stitches before pressing again.

3 Turn up the bottom hem in the same way, using a double hem but this time turning up around 15cm (6in). After pressing and tacking as before to ensure that the fabric does not slip or rumple, slipstitch the hem into place by hand. Remove the tacking stitches and press again. Now mitre the corners as described on page 30 for a neat, professional finish.

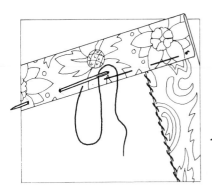

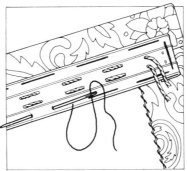

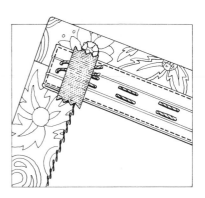

4 Turn your attention to the top of each curtain and turn down the top edge, folding it under and tacking it into place. You are now ready to apply your chosen heading tape: for the simplest type of gathers it should be around 2.5cm (1in) deep and should be positioned approximately 2cm (¾in) from the folded top of the curtain.

5 When measuring up the heading tape, allow around 3cm (1¼in) more than each curtain width and fold this overlap under at either end when tacking into place. Release the gathering cords at each end for around the last 1.5cm (½in). Tie the cords at one end into a knot and secure them temporarily at the other with sticky tape.

6 Once the heading tape is in place, machine stitch right the way around the tape, turning in the ends and stitching as you go round. Keep as straight as possible and take care not to sew down the gathering cords when you stitch the ends. Because the tape and folded fabric is bulky, it is important that it does not ruck or twist.

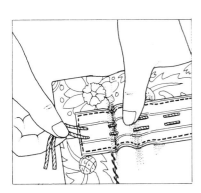

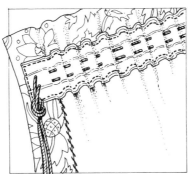

7 When you have followed this simple procedure for both curtains, remove any tacking stitching and give them a final pressing. The curtains will then be ready to gather and hang. It is important to draw the gathering cords gently from the sticky-taped end so that they do not twist or snap. Ease the fabric into regular folds as you go until they fit the required width.

8 When you have achieved the gathered effect that you want, secure the gathering cords at the end which was held by sticky tape with a loose knot. Whatever you do, do not snip off the loose ends of the cords: at some point, when it becomes necessary to take the curtains down for cleaning, you will need to release the knot and ease out the gathers to flatten the fabric once again.

9 Dress curtains can be hung from small sections of curtain track positioned as required. Alternatively, where fitting a variety of effects, they can often utilize the main rail. To give unlined curtains more weight and a better hang, thread a strip of weights into the hem before mitring the corners. Use a safety pin to ease the strip through the fabric channel. Stitch between the weights to anchor them.

lined curtains

Adding a lining to the basic curtain-making technique of the previous project involves very little extra effort, and the finished effect (opposite) more than justifies the work involved. Lined curtains will have weight and substance, they will hang beautifully, and there are practical advantages too: better heat insulation in winter, improved privacy and, of course, far more efficient screening from moonlight, sunlight or street lights. A lining will protect your curtains from dirt and dust, as well as the ageing effects of sunlight, frost and other extremes of temperature. This will prolong the life of the fabric and help keep your curtains in good condition. Lining material requires no pattern matching, so is quick and economical to make up. The linings are usually side-seamed to the curtains so they save hemming the edges too, although they can be hung separately using the curtain track.

Above: These floor-to-ceiling curtains have been lined to give a good hang and insulation from a large, draughty window. The elegantly striped fabric is cleverly co-ordinated with a matching blue and yellow floral for the draped pelmet and trellis design cushions.

MATERIALS
CURTAIN FABRIC
MATCHING THREAD
LINING FABRIC
PINS AND/OR TACKING THREAD
HEADING TAPE
CURTAIN POLE OR TRACK

Lined curtains are suitable for any room in the house, but are essential for living rooms where you need the fabric to drape and fall correctly and to have plenty of body. Even a thin, inexpensive material will look luxurious once it has been lined, especially if you are generous with the width and pleating. Lined curtains are often necessary in the bedroom too, where privacy is required, or should you prefer a darkened room. You may well desire a fuller look anyway, purely from a decorative point of view – for example, where the decorations and furnishings have been designed to create a rich look.

You can use standard inexpensive, off-white cotton lining fabric. Alternatively, for more exciting and stylish effects, co-ordinate your curtain fabric with a jewel-like plain colour in a silk or sateen-finish lining fabric. Or use a smartly subtle pinstripe: the kind of fabric sold for making up bedlinen. It can often be bought relatively cheaply and comes in usefully wide widths, which saves joining pieces together. Try to avoid the cheaper types of lining fabric, as they may shrink when the curtains are cleaned or washed.

To estimate how much lining fabric you will need for each curtain, match the width and depth of the proposed finished curtain, allowing for the depth and width of the track and the depth of your chosen heading tape as described on page 22, but not including the seam and hem allowances. Thus, when made up, the lining will be around 12cm (5in) narrower and 22.5cm (9in) shorter than the curtain itself.

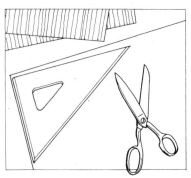

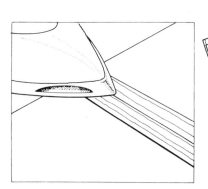

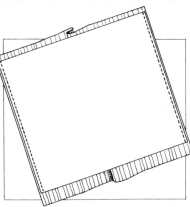

1 Estimate how much fabric you will need for the curtains and linings and cut out the appropriate number of lengths. With the main fabric you can probably draw a thread and tear it evenly, but this will not work with most lining fabrics so you will have to use sharp scissors or shears. Use a set square if you are worried about getting the fabric exactly straight.

2 Join any necessary widths or half-widths together for your curtains as described on page 34, taking care in the case of the curtain fabric to match up any patterns. Pin and then tack the widths into place. Do the same with the linings. Machine stitch the widths together using a flat seam and press open. You do not need to finish the edges.

3 Place each curtain right side up on your work surface and place a lining on top, right sides together. The top of the lining should be positioned around 7.5cm (3in) from the top of the curtain fabric and you should ensure that the side edges are lined up. Pin or tack the side edges together – there will be some slack in the curtain fabric as it is wider.

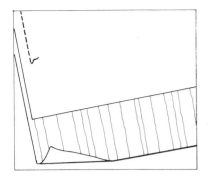

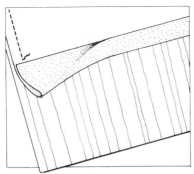

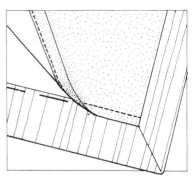

4 Machine stitch the curtain and lining fabrics together approximately 1.5cm (½in) from the edge. Start stitching from the top of the curtain and lining, and finish 15cm (6in) from the bottom edge of the lining, to allow for hems and for mitring the edges. Notch the edges of the seams to reduce any bulkiness and then press flat.

5 Next, hem the lining by turning up 5cm (2in) and pressing it to the wrong side of the lining fabric. This will allow you to make a neat double hem, 2.5cm (1in) deep. Pin or tack, and machine stitch into place. Now turn up 15cm (6in) of the main curtain fabric and press it to the wrong side, pressing the mitres in place as you go.

6 This will help you make a level double hem 7.5cm (3in) deep, which should only be tacked at this stage. The lining should now be around 5cm (2in) shorter than the curtain, which will ensure a neat finish once it is hung. From the back, this creates a kind of framework around the lining, especially with the extra allowance on the side seams and the mitred corners.

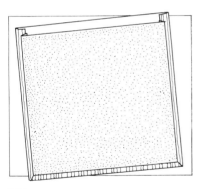

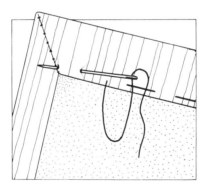

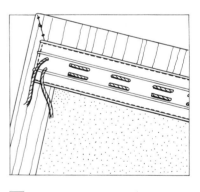

7 Now turn the lined curtain right side out. Measure to find the centre of the curtain fabric and of the lining, and mark with a pin or a notch at the top so that they can be matched together. This will create the required fabric edging around the lining on the reverse side. Slipstitch the last few centimetres (inches) of the lining at the top to the curtain fabric along the sides.

8 Hand stitch the mitred corners at the bottom of the curtain, and finish off by hemming the curtain fabric and removing the tacking threads. To finish off at the top, turn down the top 7.5cm (3in) of the curtain fabric and mitre the corners, pressing them into position. It should be possible to tack the turnover neatly over the lining.

9 Next place your chosen heading tape in position, pin, and then tack it loosely to hold it in place. Take care to remove all the pins, as they make the tape too bulky to stitch. Then trim away any excess fabric so that the raw edge will be hidden. Machine stitch the tape in place and finish off as described on page 35, steps 6 and 7.

shower curtain

If you would like your bathroom or shower room to be as stylish as the rest of your home, then finding a shower curtain that is attractive yet practical, and which co-ordinates with your other furnishings, can be like searching for a needle in a haystack. Yet making your own shower curtain is as easy as tackling the simplest unlined curtain technique, and you could create exactly the look you want for a fraction of the cost of a quality ready-made curtain. You can use plastic waterproof fabric to make the curtain; but more attractive is PVC-coated cotton (opposite) or, best of all, a polyester/cotton curtain chosen to match other furnishings and given a detachable waterproof lining. This protects the fabric from spray but still allows it to be removed easily for cleaning – an option particularly suited to en suite *baths or showers, which can then be decorated 'o match the furnishings in the bedroom.*

Above: Adding a detachable PVC lining to cotton/polyester fabric curtains offers a far wider choice of fabric for baths and showers.

MATERIALS

PLASTIC OR NYLON FABRIC
POLYESTER/COTTON CURTAIN
FABRIC (OPTIONAL)
MATCHING THREAD
STICKY TAPE AND/OR PAPER CLIPS
AND TACKING THREAD
SHEET OF TISSUE PAPER
SYNTHETIC HEADING TAPE,
DETACHABLE LINING TAPE OR
HOLE PUNCH, EYELETS AND RINGS
SHOWER ROD AND RINGS

Bathrooms and showers are always difficult rooms to decorate, but far from being another design problem to solve, shower curtains can be used to soften all those hard, shiny surfaces, to add texture and interest, and to offer the opportunity to co-ordinate something in the room with other soft furnishings such as a blind or curtain, or maybe even a chair cushion. Your choice of colour and design can be crucial: no other room in the home relies so heavily on choice of colour scheme as well as furnishings and accessories. Blue or unrelieved white and chrome can be unpleasantly cold and chilly in a dark room, whereas the correct shade of green can be comforting and an aid to relaxation. Pinks and apricots or cream can be instantly warming, while shades of butter-yellow create a cheerful atmosphere. Your choice of fabric design can have equal impact on the overall look and feel of the room. A small all-over floral immediately has an intimate cottage feel to it; stripes or a bold geometric can create a sense of light and space. Spacious rooms can even take a larger traditional design, giving a sophisticated, furnished look. Look out for fabric ranges that have already been co-ordinated with tiles, sanitaryware and bathroom accessories, to help you devise an exciting and delightful interior in what is usually one of the most neglected parts of the home.

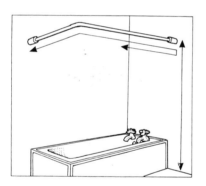

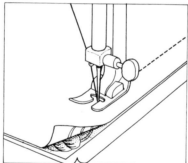

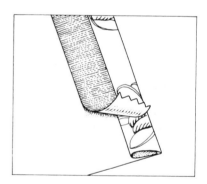

1 Fit a suitable waterproof shower rod, and then calculate the amount of fabric you require for the curtain or curtains: this should be equal to one and a half times the length of the pole or rail. Estimate the length of your curtain(s) from the top of the pole to the floor, or well inside the bath, adding 15cm (6in) for turnings top and bottom.

2 When stitching seams in plastic fabric, a sewing machine is preferable to hand stitching. Use the needle recommended for medium to heavyweight fabrics and select a long stitch to prevent the fabric puckering or tearing – small stitches would rumple the plastic. A sheet of tissue paper underneath the fabric will help to prevent it sticking to the machine presser foot.

3 Fold over the side edges by approximately 13mm (½in) to make a double hem, holding the plastic fabric in place with sticky tape while you stitch to avoid damaging the fabric with pins. Make a double hem along the lower edge in the same way, turning back around 2.5cm (1in), and along the top edge if using a plastic curtain alone.

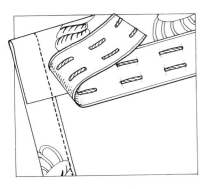

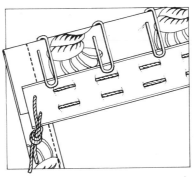

4 Plastic fabrics require a simple synthetic heading tape which is applied in the usual way. Measure the hemmed width of the curtain and allow 5cm (2in) extra at each end for turnings. Then loosen the gathering cords along the last 1.5cm (½in) or so, securing one end with a piece of sticky tape and tying the other in a knot.

5 Secure the heading tape temporarily in position on the wrong side of the fabric with sticky tape or paper clips before sewing. This avoids the use of pins and will help prevent the tape slipping out of place. Fold under the ends and machine stitch all round, taking care not to sew down the gathering cords.

6 As an alternative to heading tape, an even quicker method for hanging plastic shower curtains can be used that involves no sewing at all. Fold down a hem and, using a special eyelet punch, punch holes at each end and at regular 15cm (6in) intervals along the top of the curtain, and then insert rings in the metal-rimmed eyelets.

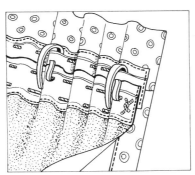

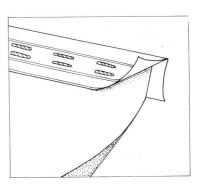

7 Shower curtains are usually attached to the overhead rail using special hooks or rings available from good haberdashery departments or bathroom centres. These perform the double rôle of curtain hooks and runners, and should move freely along the rail. They slot easily into the eyelet holes or can be fastened to split rings attached to heading tape.

8 Another option is to make a detachable plastic lining and use it in conjunction with a conventional curtain to protect it from water splashes. You should first make up a curtain in a polyester/cotton fabric of your choice (or you could use lace), following the instructions for unlined curtains on page 34.

9 Next, make up a simple lining in nylon showerproof material to match the size of your finished fabric curtain exactly, using the technique and calculations described in steps 1 to 3. Stitch a special detachable lining tape (available from haberdashery departments) to the top of this, following steps 4 and 5, and then hang the lining from the same rings as the curtain.

roller blind

A roller blind is smart and practical: it does not use a lot of material, provides efficient screening for doors and windows, and yet rolls away neatly out of sight when not in use. It is ideal where a draped or pleated effect would be too fussy, or in areas like kitchens, bathrooms or children's rooms where voluminous fabrics may be neither safe nor practical (see opposite). It is important to choose the right sort of fabric: it should be stiff enough to hang correctly and present a firm, unwrinkled finish, yet not so thick that it does not roll up easily. You can buy special ready-stiffened fabrics, including PVC and spongeable types, which are ideal for heavy-wear areas like kitchen and bathrooms. Alternatively, most fabrics can be stiffened using a wash-in, spray- or iron-on solution. You can buy everything you need – stiffener, roller, brackets, wooden batten, cord, screws and pull – either separately or in kit form.

Above: Roller blinds have been given a more formal look in this elegant interior by combining both classical and modern elements. Sunshine-yellow blinds, softened with exotic fringed shawls, brighten an otherwise austere room.

MATERIALS

BLIND FABRIC
MATCHING THREAD
PINS/OR TACKING THREAD
STIFFENER (IF REQUIRED)
ROLLER
SAW
BRACKETS
WOODEN BATTEN
CORD AND ACORN PULL
SCREWS
SET SQUARE
FABRIC ADHESIVE
STICKY TAPE
SMALL TACKS
DECORATIVE BORDER OR TRIM
(OPTIONAL)

The clean, no-fuss lines of a roller blind demand the right kind of fabric in order to be successful. You need something that is going to hang straight and crisply, and that will cope with the discipline of hard edges and a crease-free finish: definitely avoid those fabrics that love to languish in folds and pleats. Fabrics that have been specially pre-stiffened and are recommended for making roller blinds have the added advantage that they often offer a wipe-clean surface, and are also available in wider widths which avoids the necessity of making bulky joins.

However, with the option of stiffening the fabric yourself you can widen the scope for co-ordinated and creative design, provided that the chosen fabric is closely woven and has a smooth finish to ensure the right kind of look and easy rolling. You should always stiffen the fabric before cutting, as it tends to shrink; ironing is also essential, particularly after using a wash-in stiffener, but you will find that the fabric goes limp on contact, stiffening up again as it cools. For small blinds, there is an iron-on backing you can use as a stiffener.

Whatever process you choose, it is essential to use a set square to cut roller blinds to ensure they look and roll properly. For large windows, several smaller blinds will often look better than one large one, and offer the stylish option of having them pulled to varying lengths. The rollers themselves are available in wood or aluminium.

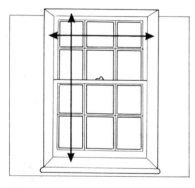

1 Accurate measurements are essential if your blind is to look right. It should hang either outside or inside the window recess. Where fitting outside the recess, allow an extra 2.5cm (1in) on either side to prevent light showing, and 5cm (2in) at the top to accommodate the roller. Blinds fitted inside the recess should be exactly to width and length.

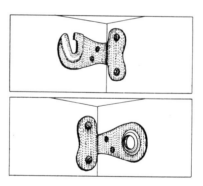

2 First screw the roller brackets into place. Now you can measure how long the roller needs to be, remembering that the square pin of the roller drops into position on the left-hand side and that the round pin is designed to slot into a hole in the right-hand side. Saw the roller to length and hammer on the appropriate pin ends.

3 Calculate how much fabric you require to cover the whole width of the roller. There is no need to allow for neatening the edges, as the stiffening process prevents them from fraying and hems would in any case be too bulky. To the length you have calculated (step 1), add around 30cm (12in) for the hem and to keep the roller covered when it is down.

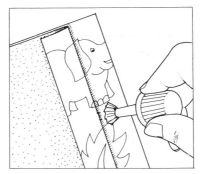

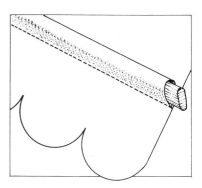

4 Should you need to join fabric widths, use a fabric adhesive and the minimum overlap after stiffening. When using a patterned fabric, you must allow enough to ensure that the design fits the blind area neatly. A set square is essential for checking that the fabric is cut at the correct angle – it will look odd if slightly askew.

5 When joining patterned fabric, fold over both pieces as necessary to achieve an exact match. Glue into the correct position with fabric adhesive. Cut the fabric to the correct size, press and stiffen as necessary.

6 Turn up 1.5cm (½in) and then 4cm (1½in) along the bottom edge to make a casing for the wooden batten. This can be glued into position or stitched using zig-zag stitch, and must be absolutely level – use a ruler and marking chalk if necessary. Cut the batten to fit and insert.

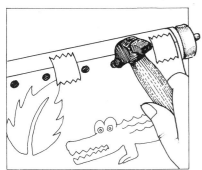

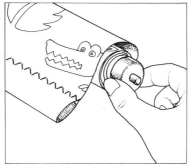

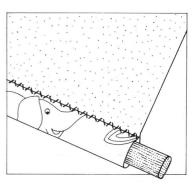

7 If you are planning to add a decorative border or trim such as lace, fringing or scallops to the bottom of the blind, the casing for the batten should be positioned higher up. Stitch or glue on your decorative hem before threading the cord through the acorn-shaped pull device and screwing the holder to the batten on the reverse of the blind.

8 To fix the other end of the fabric to the roller, check if this has been marked with a guideline. If not, mark one in with pencil to ensure that you attach the fabric completely straight. Position the fabric temporarily with sticky tape, making sure you have it rolling the right way out. Fix in position with small tacks, using a lightweight hammer.

9 It is usually necessary to adjust the tension of the roller before it will work correctly. This can be done by placing it in the brackets and pulling it down gently as far as it will go; then remove the roller from the brackets without releasing the ratchet and rewind by hand. This procedure may have to be repeated several times before the blind re-rolls smoothly.

interlined curtains

Interlining curtains can be well worth the extra time and expense involved, as the benefits are twofold. Firstly, there is the wonderful sense of thickness and luxury it brings to even a modest pair of curtains; this is especially true of longer drapes. You will find these hang much better if interlined, because they have that much extra weight and body. Secondly, there are the advantages of insulation – not just against heat loss, which can make them almost as good as double glazing, but also as a baffle against unwelcome noise and light.

Interlined curtains are usually found at windows in living rooms and bedrooms, but they are also ideally suited to hanging in front of draughty doors or French windows (opposite). A soft, loosely woven fabric is used for the interlining: either thick cotton bump or the less bulky domett, although you can use brushed cotton sheeting for an excellent budget alternative.

Above: Interlining floor-length curtains helps them to hang well and provides useful insulation. A strong rail is necessary to bear the weight of the fabric; here a handsome pole is a good choice.

CURTAIN FABRIC
MATCHING THREAD
LINING FABRIC
INTERLINING FABRIC
PINS AND/OR TACKING THREAD
HEADING TAPE
CURTAIN RAIL OR POLE

That look of luxury, and the excellent insulation benefits interlining can offer any curtain, becomes virtually compulsory when considering floor-length drapes. It can make all the difference to their hang and appearance, and you should at the very least insert a facing of interlining fabric behind the heading to give the impression of quality and body. Combined with a deep, hand-stitched pleating effect, the results can be stunning in return for a very modest outlay.

Interlining lighter, cheaper curtains will make them look more expensive and improve their performance; for better-quality furnishing fabrics it provides a superb finish and hang which is particularly important if you are planning a traditional interior. For long, winter curtains you might choose a heavy, textured-design fabric in darker, richer colours to be replaced by a lighter, fresher floral for the summer months. Dry-clean and allow the curtains to air before placing them in storage; because interlined curtains are made from three different kinds of fabric, each may need a separate cleaning technique, so specialist treatment is recommended. It also helps to keep the curtains well brushed and vacuumed while in use. This keeps dust and grime to a minimum and reduces wear. When bringing out the curtains for rehanging at the onset of colder weather first hang them outside on a fine day to freshen and allow any creases to fall out.

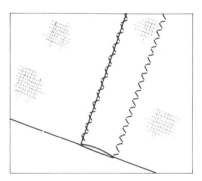

|1| First estimate and cut out the amount of fabric you need for the curtains and linings, as outlined on pages 25–27. This will tell you how much interlining fabric you will need, as this is made up to the same size. Interlining suits the more elaborate heading effects, so you may be looking at two and a half to three times your track or pole width.

|2| Join any necessary widths and half-widths together for the curtains and their linings, using a plain flat seam. Press seams open: you do not need to neaten the edges. Remember when using a patterned fabric to match any pattern repeats, and to tack the folded edges together carefully before stitching as described on page 34.

|3| Cut out the interlining fabric to match the curtain lengths. Because the fabric used is generally loosely woven, you can join widths with a lapped seam using two rows of zig-zag stitch. With the curtain fabric right side down, position the interlining on the wrong side of the fabric, matching the sides and lower edges.

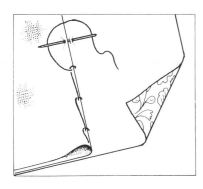

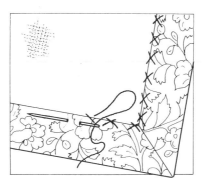

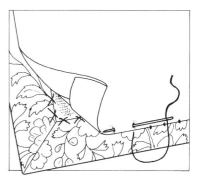

4 Once in position, fold back the interlining fabric and lockstitch it into place. Work two rows of lockstitch for every width of fabric used, with the stitching running from top to bottom of the curtain length, to ensure that the interlining and the curtain fabric stay together once they are hanging.

5 Turn in the curtain fabric and interlining together along the side edges by about 5cm (2in). Tack into position, then herringbone stitch. Turn up the interlining and curtain fabric along the lower edge in the same way and herringbone stitch this too. For a neat finish, mitre the corners as described on page 30.

6 Now lay the lining fabric on top of the interlining and tack, then lockstitch the two together. It may be necessary to trim the lining fabric to the same size as the curtain. Fold under the lining by 2.5cm (1in) at the sides and bottom of the curtain and tack, then slipstitch it into position. Do not mitre the corners.

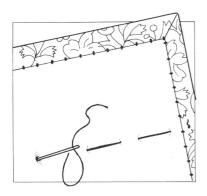

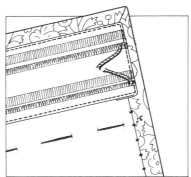

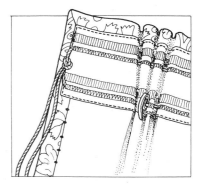

7 To ensure that the lining and interlining stay in place while the heading tape is being applied, tack a line of loose stitches across the curtain about 15–20cm (6–8in) from the top. If you use tailor's chalk and a yardstick or rigid metre (yard) rule to draw in the line first you can be sure that it is straight.

8 Cut your chosen heading tape to fit, allowing about 1.5cm (½in) at each end for turning under. Pin, then tack it into position approximately 6mm (¼in) from the top edge of the curtain. Machine stitch the tape, starting at the top edge, then the lower edge in the same direction, and finally the sides, to prevent puckering.

9 Remove the tacking stitches and press the curtain. Then draw out the gathering cords at each end of the tape and make a firm knot in one end. Insert sufficient curtain hooks into the tape and then gently pull the cords, easing the gathers into even pleats. Secure the cords with a knot at the other end, but do not cut.

frilled curtains

Where you might be looking to add a little extra decorative detail to a curtain or pair of curtains, a modest frill in matching fabric along the inside edge is ideal. It is pretty without being too showy and gives both simple lined and unlined curtains a professional finish (see opposite). This is an effect that would suit any room, especially where you are planning to use other co-ordinated soft furnishings that might feature frills, such as cushion covers or a bed valance. It also looks lovely with fresh floral fabrics.

However, should you prefer something with a little more decorative impact, you can easily expand on this idea to make a larger or more dramatic double frilled edging. You might use a different, even contrasting fabric for the frills, or add a matching frilled pelmet and tie-backs to complete the picture.

Above: A pretty checked fabric has been used here to make a pair of fixed curtains, held back by matching fabric bows. The frill detail attached to the inside edge completes the decorative effect perfectly.

MATERIALS

CURTAIN AND FRILL FABRIC
MATCHING THREAD
BIAS BINDING (FOR DOUBLE
FRILLS ONLY)
PINS AND/OR TACKING THREAD
HEADING TAPE
CURTAIN RAIL OR POLE

If you want to make the most of a frilled edging on your curtains – playing it up rather than just using it as an attractive finishing touch – you might consider using a different fabric to the main curtains. For a subtle touch, this could be a co-ordinated design from the same fabric range, maybe in a different but complementary colourway, or it could be in the same shade but to a different scale or design. Alternatively, go for a really bold contrast, perhaps choosing a plain colour to complement a busy patterned fabric, or a patterned frill to decorate plain fabric curtains. To add impact, you could choose a stronger colour: say, shades of red or purple to highlight a pink curtain, or orange or gold to edge a yellow one.

As well as being highly decorative, a frill can be used to great practical advantage: for example if you have moved to a new home, or if you wish to use the curtains in a different room to make way for a new window effect, and they are not quite big enough. Letting out hems and seams is fiddly and not always successful if the fabric has faded or changed colour slightly, and you will certainly not want the curtains to look skimped, so add a frill to sides and hem to extend them cleverly and give the curtains an instant new look. Choose a suitable fabric for the frill and make up as described, slipstitching invisibly to the edges and/or lower edge of your existing curtains as required. These instructions are for adding frills to unlined curtains.

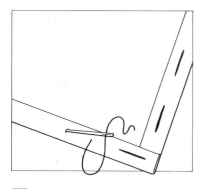

1 Measure and cut out your curtain fabric as described on page 34, step 1, and join any widths, using a flat fell seam so that the raw edges are enclosed. Fold over the two side edges and the lower hem by approximately 1.5cm (½in) and tack. Measuring around the curtain will give you the length of fabric you require for the frill.

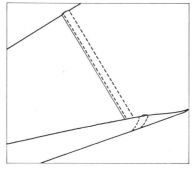

2 The frill needs to be at least one and a half times, and preferably twice, the length and bottom hem of the curtain. Width will be determined by the proposed width of the frill: for a frill approximately 7.5cm (3in) wide, you will need a strip of fabric 10cm (4in) wide. These strips can be joined if necessary, using French seams.

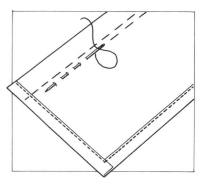

3 Hem the side and the bottom edges of the strip with a 6mm (¼in) double hem, first tacking, then machine stitching. To gather the strip into a frill, run two rows of gathering stitches 1.5cm (½ in) from the top edge. Working along the strip in sections will help distribute the gathers evenly along the length of the frill.

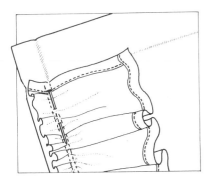

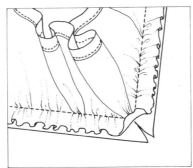

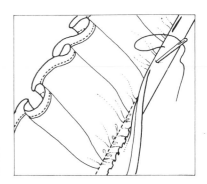

4 You will need to turn down a hem of around 2.5cm (1in) along the top edge of the curtain and press the fold in order to accommodate the heading tape and to avoid positioning the frill too high. You can now open up the hem allowances you made at the sides and start pinning the frill to the fold line, right sides together.

5 Tack the frill into position along the line of gathering stitches, making sure you adjust it frequently so that the gathers are evenly distributed, but with plenty of fullness at the corners. This will encourage the frill to hang well. Clip the fabric curve of the corner to ensure that it does not look too bulky.

6 Trim the raw edges of the frill to 6mm (¼in) and turn over the hem allowance of the curtain fabric to make a bound edge. Tack and press this towards the curtain fabric, and topstitch into position on the right side of the curtain. Apply the appropriate heading tape as described on page 35, steps 5 and 6.

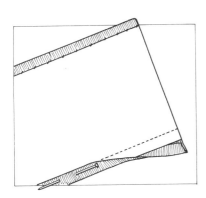

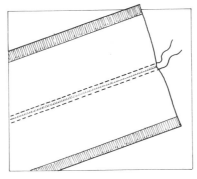

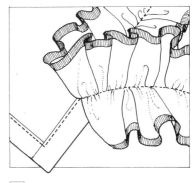

7 To make a more elaborate-looking double frill, cut the strips of fabric on the straight grain to the required length, joining any widths with French seams as before. Stitch 6mm (¼in) double hems along the sides, or maybe bind them with a contrasting colour of bias binding to create an even more dramatic impact.

8 Now fold the strip of fabric in half lengthwise and press the fold, before working two rows of gathering stitches about 3mm (⅛in) either side of the fold line. If you work in sections of around 91.5cm (36in) at a time you will find the gathers easier to control. Make up the curtain following step 1.

9 Pin and then tack the centre of the frill to the right side of the curtain, following the line of the machine stitching on the hems. Machine stitch into place and remove the gathering stitches. Turn over the top edge of the curtain on the fold line and apply your chosen heading tape following the instructions on page 35, steps 5 and 6.

café curtains

Café curtains are a special type of permanent curtain that is hung from a pole or rail and cover only the lower half of the window. Their main purpose is to provide privacy or to hide an unwelcome view, and they can offer a far more attractive and less expensive option than obscured glass in the bathroom or kitchen. Being made from ordinary curtain fabric, they create a quite different effect from nets or screens which remain opaque. Unlined café curtains do allow some light to filter through during the day, whereas lined curtains are more substantial; the quality and thickness of the fabric you use will make a difference to hang and appearance, too. The curtain headings can be decoratively scalloped or tabbed and are either slotted directly on to the slender pole or rail, or hung via metal rings. In the photograph opposite fabric has been shirred on to a free-standing folding frame to create an unusual café curtain. While not creating a totally flat effect, café curtains do not feature dense gathers, although the scalloped headings can sometimes be hand pleated.

Above: Tab-headed café curtains hung from a narrow rail and used in conjunction with a matching roller blind provides a flexible system for covering the window. Lace curtains and blinds work well with co-ordinated dress curtains like these.

MATERIALS
CURTAIN FABRIC
MATCHING THREAD
PAPER PATTERN
LINING FABRIC (OPTIONAL)
PINS AND/OR TACKING THREAD
CURTAIN POLE
CURTAIN RINGS (OPTIONAL)

Café curtains may seem to offer a rather limited window effect reserved for screening the lower panes, but in fact the design potential is limitless and has a wide range of useful applications. The curtains themselves might be frilled or plain and feature a choice of heading effects from tabs and scallops to simple ruching. You can also influence the final look simply by your choice of finish or fabric.

Stripes are smart and in pastel Neopolitan ice-cream shades will create a cool, Continental look, while flounced florals look pretty and old-fashioned and are the perfect companions for stripped pine, brass rails and other traditional furnishing touches. Because the curtains do not feature heavy pleating or gathering, they are also suitable for pictorial design fabrics which may be ideal for kitchens or children's rooms. As a charming alternative to nets, use lace to make up the curtains where only partial screening is required. Frills, fringes and other trimmings are useful for adding interest along the lower hem, but can also be applied around all four sides of the curtain and used in conjunction with conventional simple heading tape as a softer alternative to the tabbed and scalloped style.

Often designed to be kept permanently closed, a pair of café curtains that can be drawn to the sides is more flexible yet still attractive, especially when used in conjunction with matching full-length curtains.

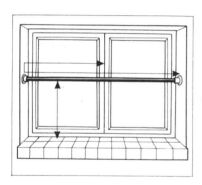

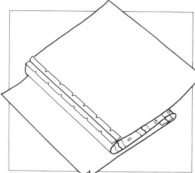

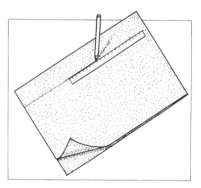

1 Fabric for unlined café curtains is calculated at around one and a half times the length of the pole. The length of the curtain is usually measured to just touching the windowsill, plus 7.5cm (3in) to turn up at the bottom and allowing sufficient fabric to make your chosen heading – such as the depth of the scallops – plus 7.5cm (3in) for the top hem.

2 Begin by cutting out and making up the curtain, joining widths and matching any pattern where necessary, using the technique described for unlined curtains on page 34, steps 1 to 3. To create a scallop-shaped heading for café curtains, you will need to make a paper pattern cut to the same width as your curtain and 30.5cm (12in) deep.

3 Fold your paper pattern in half, and then draw a straight line around 7.5cm (3in) from the top. Mark out the scallops, starting at the fold line in the centre, to ensure that they look even. The scallops should be around 15cm (6in) in diameter and about 4cm (1½in) apart, but this will have to be adjusted to fit the space available.

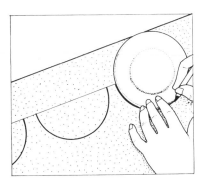

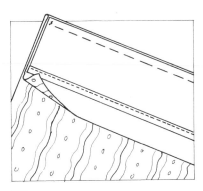

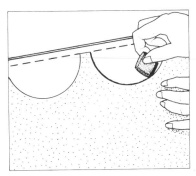

4 The easiest and most reliable way to draw your scallop shapes is to use a circular object such as a plate or a pair of compasses, and to use your line as the centre point for a regular semi-circular shape. If you are planning to hand pleat between each scallop, you will have to allow more space between them – and more fabric.

5 For a smart, professional finish, you should face the heading. Cut a 15cm (6in) strip of fabric to the same width as the curtain: this can be the same or lining fabric. Turn up a 1.5cm (½in) double hem across the lower edge of the facing. Match the facing to the top of the curtain, right sides together, and tack into place top and bottom.

6 To mark the scallops on to the curtain, fold over the top edge of the curtain on the right side to the depth of the scallop plus 7.5cm (3in) to allow for a hem. Place your paper pattern along the folded edge at the top and draw around the scallop shapes using tailor's chalk. Machine stitch all around this chalk line.

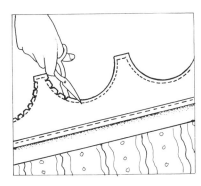

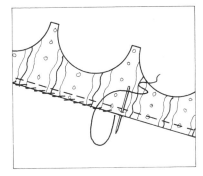

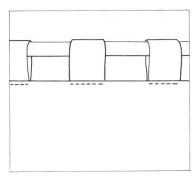

7 You can now cut around all the scallops approximately 6mm (¼in) from the stitching line. Clipping around the curves and corners using a sharp pair of scissors will ensure that the fabric is flat when turned the right way out. Turn the facing to the wrong side of the curtain and press carefully, easing out the shapes.

8 Turn under a 1.5cm (½in) double hem along the edge of the fabric and hemstitch into place. Hand sew metal or wooden curtain rings to the centre of each scallop to enable the curtain to be attached freely to the pole. Now press a double hem along the bottom of the curtain, tack to hold in place and stitch to finish, mitring the corners.

9 Alternative heading ideas for café curtains include pinch pleating each scallop by hand (see page 23), for which you need to add 8cm (3¼in) to the width of fabric required for each space between the scallops, or you can apply a tab heading by stitching fabric loops to the head of the curtain in matching fabric and threading on to the pole.

curtain headings

You can achieve so many different and exciting curtain effects simply through your choice of heading or gathering. The more elaborate styles may be more expensive or time-consuming to make, but the results can be stunning, so you may feel that they are well worth it for the right setting. The deeper headings and more decorative gathers can give a room a real sense of luxury and quality, while the curtains will have that professional hand-finished look. A fine pole and rings draw attention to the curtain headings. The curtain headings shown opposite have been highlighted further with matching ribbons.

While you can achieve all this simply by applying one of the superior types of heading tape, a completely hand-stitched pleating effect looks really classy. A good-quality fabric, well-lined curtains and hand-made pinch or box pleats are an unbeatable combination if you are seeking the very best in window dressing. These are not particularly difficult to apply: they simply require careful and accurate measuring and a little patience.

Above: Pinch pleats are an elegant choice for grander window effects and are easily achieved with a little patience and attention to detail. They can be hand-made or gathered using special drawstring tapes.

MATERIALS
MADE-UP CURTAINS
MATCHING THREAD
PINS AND/OR TACKING THREAD
STICKY TAPE
HEADING TAPE (OPTIONAL)
CURTAIN TRACK OR POLE

While the simplest heading tapes, with their lack of depth and modest gathers, do little for good-quality, heavyweight fabrics, one of the more sophisticated effects like pinch or pencil pleats can do wonders for some inexpensive materials, especially if you add lining or interlining to give body and weight to the hang of the curtains. This can be a good way to achieve a more exciting or expensive-looking window effect if you are working to a strict budget. Plenty of width and extravagant gathers immediately suggest a sense of luxury, especially if the curtains are allowed to tumble right to the floor. This treatment will make something of even the cheapest fabrics like gauzy muslin, home-dyed sheeting or lining fabric, provided you allow extra width and gather masses of it.

Never try to economize by buying a more expensive fabric and skimping on volume. Curtains that barely cover the window frame or which cheat on the width required for the heading never look good and your penny-pinching will immediately be obvious, ruining the look of the whole room. Apart from lack of gathers, the cheaper tapes do not give any depth or impact to the top of your curtains, and even if this will be hidden behind a pelmet, the extra body provided is important for a good hang. Some of the better-quality tapes are stiffened; alternatively, add an interfacing between the tape and curtain fabric to give it the necessary weight.

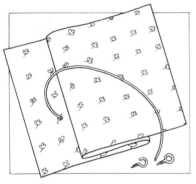

1 The simplest type of heading for informal curtains that do not require a lot of gathering, or nets and café curtains, is a machine-stitched casing through which a narrow curtain rod or plastic-covered wire is threaded. You will need no more than one and a half times the width of the window in fabric. Allow 12cm (5in) for the heading.

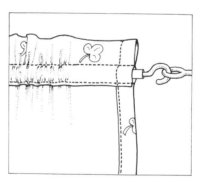

2 When the rest of the curtain has been made up, turn over the top and tack it to create a double hem approximately 5cm (2in) deep. Topstitch into place using two lines of machine stitching about 2.5cm (1in) apart, with the top row 2.5cm (1in) from the top of the curtain to create some gather once threaded on to its wire or pole.

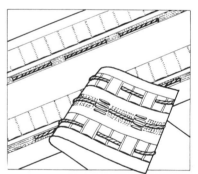

3 Curtain heading tapes are equally simple to apply and come in a wide choice of sizes and pleating styles. Be sure to buy sufficient fabric to accommodate your chosen gathering, as this can vary considerably. It is important to position the tape absolutely straight at the top of the fabric or the curtain will hang askew.

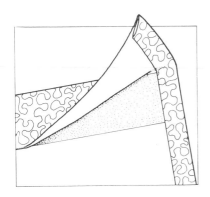

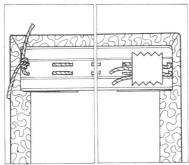

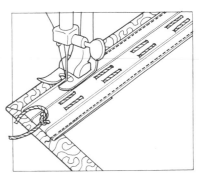

4 The cheaper, simpler types of heading tape are not stiffened, so it may be worth applying a 5cm (2in) strip of iron- or sew-on interfacing to give the top of the curtain a little more body before you stitch on the tape. All styles of heading tape are applied in the same way: allow 3cm (1¼in) more than the curtain width for turning under.

5 When the tape has been pinned and tacked to the top of the curtain, the gathering cords in the last 1.5cm (½in) at each end should be teased out and tied in a knot at one end. Secure the other end with a piece of sticky tape. A few hooks inserted at this stage will allow you to hang the curtain temporarily and check the effect.

6 Machine stitch in place; if you work along the top edge first and then the lower edge the stitching will run in the same direction, and this prevents the tape from rucking up. Finish the side edges. Insert the hooks and draw up the gathers, spreading them out evenly across the width of the curtain. Secure the cords but do not cut off.

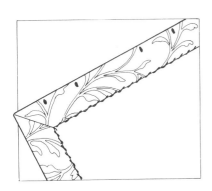

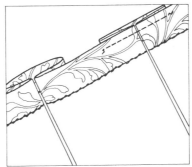

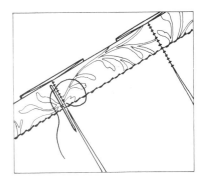

7 You can hand stitch both pencil and pinch pleats with superb results, but one effect that does not have the easier option of heading tapes is box pleats. Calculate the fabric as outlined on page 23 and mark the positions of the folds across the fabric. The first two marks should be 5cm (2in) and 10cm (4in) respectively from the edge.

8 Next make alternate marks 10cm (4in) and 5cm (2in) across the curtain until you reach the other side, which again will have two marks at 5cm (2in) intervals. Start at a mark 20.5cm (8in) from one end and join this to the next mark 20.5cm (8in) away. Pin and tack. Leave a space of 10cm (4in), then join the next 20.5cm (8in) sections together.

9 When you have repeated this sequence across the curtain, flatten the pleats, pin them, and then hand or machine stitch. Begin stitching the front pleats only, starting about 2cm (¾in) from the top of the curtain down to around 8cm (3¼in). Slipstitch the back of the pleats right through the lining to the main fabric.

roman blind

A Roman blind is the perfectly elegant option for rooms where curtains are too fussy or impractical and a roller blind would look a little too stark, or simply not classy enough. It is a style that particularly suits plain fabrics and understated interiors, as shown opposite. The fabric does not have to be stiffened like that for roller blinds, but something of sufficient weight is essential if the blind is to fold and hang correctly. It is usually lined with sateen curtain lining fabric in order to give the blind some thickness and body.

A Roman blind can be positioned either inside or outside the window recess, and is raised in a series of smart horizontal folds by means of a side-operated series of cords and rings. You can buy all the components you need in kit form.

Above: Here a Roman blind has been used in conjunction with richly patterned, heavily lined curtains and a draped fabric pelmet to create a sumptuous dining room. The same golden fabric as the blind has been used to line the curtains and pelmet.

MATERIALS
BLIND FABRIC
LINING FABRIC
MATCHING THREAD
PINS AND/OR TACKING THREAD
WOODEN BATTEN
AUSTRIAN/ROMAN BLIND TAPES
STRONG NYLON CORD
METAL RINGS
WINDOW HEADER BOARD
SCREW EYES
TACKS OR STAPLES
CLEAT

The tailored effect of a Roman blind is smart and distinctive, and completely different from any other blind or curtain look. It is perfect for situations where you do not want too many frills and gathers, yet is not as austere as a roller blind. Fully extended, the effect is one of a flat panel, but because this is not tautly stiffened it has a softer look. The precise horizontal pleats created by the gathering cords look good when the blind is raised to any level at the window and this style usually has at least a couple of pleats left down to show off its best features. The operating cord is secured by a cleat fastened to the wall. Up or down, it is essential to use a fabric that can be well ironed and which does not crease easily. A large window often looks better with several smaller blinds, rather than one large one which can start to sag over wider widths. These might be drawn to different levels for both practical and visual effect.

While the uncluttered concertina effect looks particularly good with plain fabrics, Roman blinds can be used equally successfully with patterns, especially when used with matching dress curtains. Another way to make them a little more decorative but without losing that tailored look, is to add a band or border, usually at the bottom edge of the blind. Braid, ribbon or fringes are all suitable or, for a slightly softer look, you could add an appliqué, lace or embroidered hem.

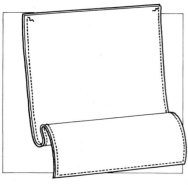

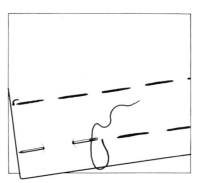

1 First cut out your blind and lining fabric to the required size, allowing 2.5cm (1in) on the width for side seams and 15cm (6in) on the length for turnings top and bottom. Place the fabrics right sides together and tack to prevent them slipping. Then machine stitch both the sides and bottom to provide a 1.5cm (½in) seam. Turn the blind the right way out and press.

2 Working on the reverse of the blind, use a rigid rule and sharpened tailor's chalk to mark the two lines that will enclose the batten, about 14cm (5½in) from the bottom edge. Space them so that the batten will slide into the casing easily. If it is too tight the fabric will pucker and not hang properly. Tack along the casing lines.

3 Next mark in the vertical lines that will show the position of the gathering tapes, again using tailor's chalk and making sure that the lines are straight and parallel on the fabric. The tapes should start and finish about 1.5cm (½in) from the edges of the blind and be regularly spaced around 30.5cm (12in) apart.

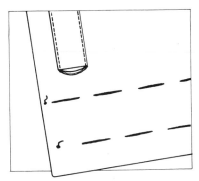

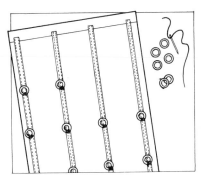

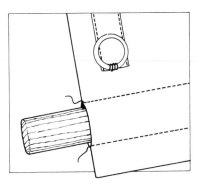

4 Using your marks as a guideline, tack and then stitch the tapes into position, stitching along both edges of each tape and sewing through the blind fabric and the lining. Make sure that there is a horizontal loop at the bottom of each tape, and keep the line of stitches as even as possible. Turn under the raw edges top and bottom.

5 The metal rings that take the gathering cords must be sewn on to the tapes by hand. The first should be positioned approximately 1.5cm (½in) from the top of the batten casing, and the rest evenly spaced along the tape at intervals of 15cm (6in). It is very important that the rows of rings match up horizontally across the tapes.

6 Once all the rings are firmly in position, machine stitch along the lines intended to enclose the batten casing. Cut the flat timber batten supplied exactly to length, then, by unpicking the stitches at one end, insert it into the casing. Slipstitch the ends of fabric together again, leaving the batten completely enclosed.

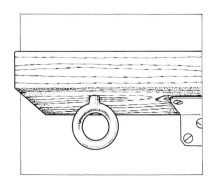

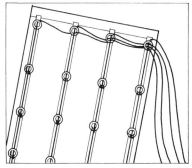

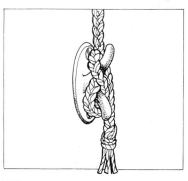

7 You will need a section of window header board cut exactly to fit the width of the blind and measuring 2.5 x 5cm (1 x 2in). Fasten this to the top of the window and insert the screw eyes which are designed to correspond with each vertical row of rings. A larger screw will be needed at one end to take the weight of the main pulling cord.

8 Cut the nylon cord into lengths twice the length of the blind plus once its width to take them to the edge for pulling. Laying the blind flat, tie these cords to the bottom rings and then thread them through each ring in a row. Tack or staple the blind to the top board, so that each length of cord can be taken through the right screw eye.

9 When all the rows are correctly threaded, the cords can be knotted together approximately 2.5cm (1in) from the outside edge of the blind. They can be plaited or cut level, and then knotted again nearer the ends. Fasten a cleat to the wall beside the blind and use it to hold the cords secure whenever the blind is raised.

austrian blind

Sometimes called a festoon blind, Austrian blinds are flouncy and frilly, the fabric ruched and gathered into elaborate swags. The blinds are constructed using a system of cords and rings as with Roman blinds, but produce a much softer, more fussy effect that is dressy enough to be used alone at the window, but which is often combined with matching curtains. As shown opposite, Austrian blinds in plain fabric are smart and elegant in a room furnished in neutral shades. They usually feature a pleated heading like curtains and are fastened to a heading board.

The best kinds of fabrics to use for Austrian blinds are lightweight so that they drape and gather well. The blind can be left gathered to any point on the window during the day; if you are planning to leave it mostly down, like a form of screening, choose sheer or semi-sheer fabrics so that light can filter through. Weights inserted in the lower hem of the blind at the bottom of each length of vertical tape will help lightweight fabrics to hang well.

Above: The Austrian blind is often used in conjunction with matching curtains, tie-backs and valance to create a total look that particularly suits larger windows. This is an excellent way to make any window a stunning focal point.

MATERIALS
BLIND FABRIC
MATCHING THREAD
AUSTRIAN BLIND TAPES
PINS AND/OR TACKING THREAD
METAL RINGS
NYLON CORD
HEADING TAPE
WINDOW HEADER BOARD
SCREW EYES
CURTAIN TRACK
CLEAT

Because they are unmistakably dressy, Austrian blinds must be used judiciously around the home. The effect may be showy and professional looking but it is relatively simple to achieve, especially if you use one of the kits available which include all the tapes, cords and rings you need. Flushed with success and enthusiasm, the amateur home furnisher might easily be encouraged to put them everywhere. However, a large flounced blind in too many rooms can be a little overpowering – rather like eating a whole box of chocolates in one sitting! Save them for where they can be employed to best use and most creatively.

Austrian blinds are excellent used as the perfect compromise between blind and curtains, say in a bathroom or kitchen where you do not want the fabric to extend beyond the window recess, but would prefer a softer, more gathered look than a roller blind. The festoon's generous pleats and softly curved swags are ideal for offsetting the rather functional effect of bathroom sanitaryware and kitchen appliances.

An Austrian blind is also an excellent way to dress a large, imposing window – or to make an insigificant one look more important. Select a bold or soft floral design, give it plenty of gathers and scalloped edges, and co-ordinate with an elaborately frilled pelmet, dress curtains and matching tie-backs for an eye-catching focal point in living room, formal dining room or even a rather grand bedroom.

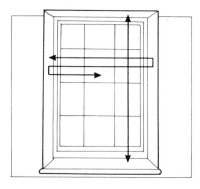

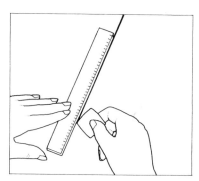

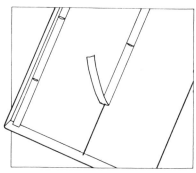

1 Estimate the fabric at two to two and a half times the width of the window – the blind can be positioned either inside or outside the window recess. Allow 2.5cm (1in) on the width for seams and add 22.5cm (9in) to the length for turnings and hems. If you need to join widths, allow 2.5cm (1in) for each seam.

2 Cut the fabric to size using a set square to ensure that the blind will hang straight. Join any lengths as necessary and hem the sides and bottom as described for unlined curtains, page 34, steps 1 to 3. Lay the fabric flat, wrong side up, and mark in the position of the vertical tapes at regular intervals using a rigid ruler and tailor's chalk.

3 The more tapes you have, the more swags you will create. They should be at least 25.5cm (10in) wide, and no more than 61cm (24in) apart (for large windows), remembering that the distance between them will be halved when the blind is gathered. Where fabric lengths have been joined, try to position the tapes over the seams.

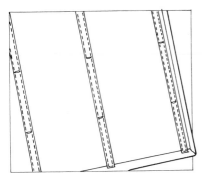

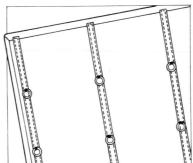

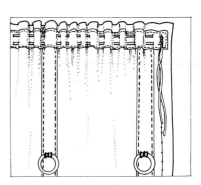

4 Tack and then machine stitch the tapes into position, stitching down both sides of each tape as described for Roman blinds, and ensuring that the loops are aligned across the fabric with a horizontal loop at the bottom of each tape. The ends of the tapes should be folded under by about 6mm (¼in) and machine stitched into place.

5 Hand stitch the rings for the gathering cords on to the tapes, the first positioned approximately 20.5cm (8in) from the top of the blind and the last no less than 20.5cm (8in) from the bottom edge. Place the others between at regular intervals of about 20.5cm (8in), making sure that they are aligned across the tapes horizontally.

6 Apply the curtain heading tape of your choice to the wrong side of the top edge of the blind, having folded it over around 1.5cm (½in) and following the instructions on page 35, steps 5 and 6. Pull the cords and adjust the gathers until the blind fits the width of your window, and then insert curtain hooks into the tape at 7.5cm (3in) intervals.

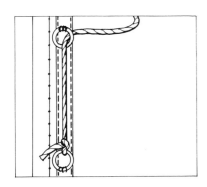

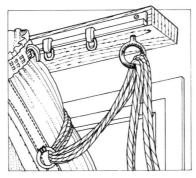

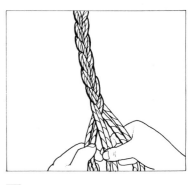

7 Cut a piece of 2.5 x 5cm (1 x 2in) window header board to width and fasten to the top of the window, attaching screw eyes to the underside of the board to correspond with the rows of rings. Cut the cords to size as described for Roman blinds, page 67, step 8. Then lay the blind flat, tie them to the bottom rings and thread through each ring in the row.

8 Attach a length of curtain track to the header board and hang the blind from it. Thread the cords through the relevant screw eyes, starting at the side of the blind opposite to where you are going to position the retaining cleat on the wall. Knot the cords together at the far end, leaving sufficient for the blind to work easily.

9 Do not cut off the cords after knotting, as they will have to be released and the blind let out should you wish to clean it. Instead, twist or plait the excess cords together and knot the end loosely. Fasten a cleat hook to the wall next to the blind and use it to secure the cords when the blind is raised up the window.

tie-backs

Curtain tie-backs are essentially a practical device for keeping open curtains out of the way where they might be dangerous or a nuisance, such as in the kitchen or bathroom, or for holding back heavy drapes to let in more light during the day. But they have also become a highly decorative feature, an opportunity to experiment with co-ordinated window accessories and to create a more complex and exciting window effect.

You can buy tasselled cords which make perfectly serviceable tie-backs, but it is far more fun – and looks more professional – to make your own from matching or co-ordinated fabric. The scope for style and decoration is unlimited: tie-backs can be stiffened or lined, straight or shaped, bordered, frilled or ruffled. They can be as simple or ostentatious as you like, and take very little time and fabric to make. Fringed and interlined tie-backs, as shown opposite, are ideal for restraining heavy drapes. Rings stitched to the tie-backs are fastened to a wall hook to secure.

Above: There are many ways a tie-back can complement your curtains: instead of using matching fabrics use a contrasting one as here, attractively decorated with a co-ordinated rosette and covered button detail.

MATERIALS
FABRIC TO MATCH OR
CO-ORDINATE WITH CURTAINS
MATCHING THREAD
PAPER PATTERN (OPTIONAL)
PINS AND/OR TACKING THREAD
LINING FABRIC
INTERFACING
BUMP OR INTERLINING FABRIC
(OPTIONAL)
HEADING TAPE
(FOR RUFFLED TIE-BACK)
METAL RINGS
WALL HOOKS
PIPING CORD (OPTIONAL)
BIAS BINDING (OPTIONAL)

Tie-backs can be useful not just for holding back conventional curtains, but also as a decorative element to create a different look for dress curtains, or to hold them away from the blind or shade which actually covers the window.

Another creative way to use tie-backs is where the curtains are fixed in some way and need to be swept back partially to prevent them covering the window during the day. This is not only essential for letting in light, but also creates a dramatic, sweeping shape which can be quite different from the usual draped effect. A pair of floor-length curtains can sometimes be joined at the top, maybe with a large central bow or rosette, and then swept back to either side – this strongly traditional look suits tall, elegant windows. For a more up-to-date look, fix a single curtain or pair of curtains along top and sides and use a tie-back device to hook the lower corners back like sails: a contrasting lining will emphasize the effect. Finally, a single curtain can look far more interesting and impressive than the conventional pair if fixed along the top and swept to one side by means of a wide, interlined tie-back.

All these treatments are useful for reducing large expanses of window glass to create a more intimate atmosphere. But do not forget the opportunity for using tie-backs in other situations: essential to hold back the shower curtain when not in use, or for drapes around a four-poster or half-tester bed.

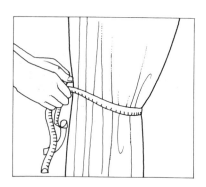

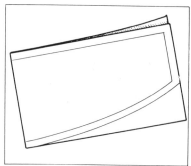

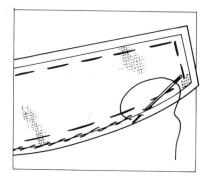

1 To calculate how much fabric you require to make tie-backs, use a piece of string or a tape to measure how much it will take to embrace the fullness of the curtain and still reach the wall. The width will be relevant to the size and style of your curtains, but most are around 12cm (5in) deep. Add 1.5cm (½in) all round for turning under.

2 Cut out two strips of fabric to the required measurements for each tie-back. If you fancy making a curved and shaped style, draw a paper pattern with a suitably sweeping shape on folded paper (for symmetry), half the required length and allowing 1.5cm (1in) all round for turnings. Cut out, unfold and test it around the curtain.

3 Cut a piece of interfacing to the finished size of your tie-backs and tack it to the wrong side of one of the lengths, making sure it is positioned centrally. Catchstitch in place. To give tie-backs body and a thick, luxurious look, you can insert a piece of bump or interlining fabric underneath the interfacing before you sew.

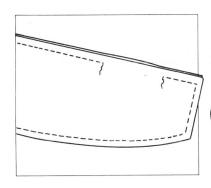

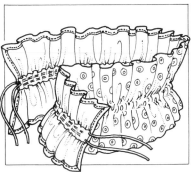

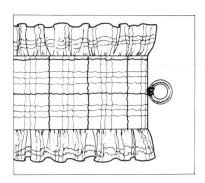

4 Place the second piece of fabric on to the interfaced tie-back, right sides together. With bulky fabrics like velvet, use lining sateen for the reverse side of the tie-back. Pin together, tack and machine stitch all round using the 1.5cm (½in) allowance. Leave an opening of approximately 10cm (4in) along one of the long sides.

5 Clip the corners so that they lie flat, then turn the tie-back the right way out. Press and slipstitch to close the opening. For a ruffled tie-back, make up to twice the required length and sew simple curtain heading tape along the centre of the reverse side. Pull and fasten the cords to gather the tie-back to the required length.

6 Adding a frill makes the tie-back even more decorative, and it can be co-ordinated with other frilled soft furnishings such as cushions, curtains and valance. You must allow two extra pieces of fabric for each tie-back, at least one and a half times the length of the tie-back fabric and twice your chosen frill width plus 1.5cm (½in).

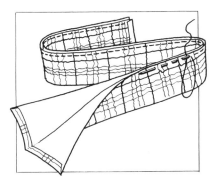

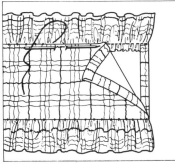

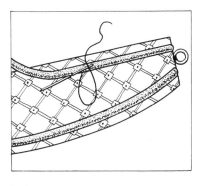

7 Fold the fabric for the frill in half lengthways, wrong sides together. Sew a double row of gathering stitches 6mm (¼in) and 1.5cm (½in) from the raw edges. Gently pull through the threads, taking care they do not snap, and adjust the gathers so that the frill is the same length as the tie-back. Machine stitch in place.

8 Turn under the 1.5cm (½in) allowance all round the top piece of fabric intended for your tie-back and slipstitch the frill into position. Turn under the short ends and slipstitch these into place also. Turn under the allowance on the tie-back backing fabric and slipstitch this to the frilled section, wrong sides together.

9 Another decorative option which looks smart rather than frilly is to add a piped detail along the edge of your tie-backs. Piping cord is available in different thicknesses: use number 2 or 3 and cover with a bias binding strip 4cm (1½in) wide. Slipstitch to the front section of the tie-back instead of a frill (see step 8).

valance pelmet

A flounced fabric pelmet at the head of your window is the perfect 'finishing touch' for your curtains. This gathered valance is no more trouble to make than a miniature curtain – indeed, the technique is more or less the same – yet it can make all the difference to the overall look of your window. You can use a pelmet to disguise its true dimensions: a deep pelmet will make a window look shorter and more square, while a high one used in conjunction with long curtains, as shown opposite, may create the illusion of elegant length. A fabric pelmet can offer other practical advantages too: it hides the rail and the curtain heading, and can protect the top of your curtains from dust and dirt.

The valance can be fixed to a pelmet board at the top of the window or hung from a rail positioned in front of the curtain track. It is usually lined to give it good body and hang and may even be interlined or stiffened with an interfacing.

Above: A rosette detail complements a fabric valance.

MATERIALS
FABRIC TO MATCH OR
CO-ORDINATE WITH CURTAINS
MATCHING THREAD
PINS AND/OR TACKING THREAD
LINING FABRIC
INTERLINING OR INTERFACING
(OPTIONAL)
CURTAIN HOOKS
PELMET BOARD AND EYELET RINGS
OR CURTAIN RAIL
HEADING TAPE

While a fabric pelmet planned as part of a complete window effect looks stunning, it can also be added later to an existing pair of curtains to create interest and a new look without spending a lot of time or money. If you cannot find a suitable fabric to match or co-ordinate with the existing curtain fabric, then a deep plain colour in some contrasting or complementary shade can be most effective, especially if you use the same fabric to add a border along the sides and hem of your curtains to tie in the effect.

A valance pelmet also offers scope for co-ordinated effects, not just with your curtains, but also with other fabric accessories in the room. In the bedroom it could be matched to a bed valance, or to the frill around a dressing table or bedside tablecloth. In the bathroom you could add a frilled valance around a vanity basin, shirr matching fabric behind the glass in a bathroom cabinet, or even make a matching pelmet to hide your shower rail. You can vary the effect at the window too, by using several pelmets of different depths to create a layered effect – very Victorian if hung with fringes and trimmings – or by curving the lower edge of a single pelmet to create an arched effect over the window. For very grand windows, the valance might be ruched as well as gathered into a series of deep swags to help maintain the right balance – with floor-to-ceiling curtains the pelmet should ideally cover one-sixth of the window.

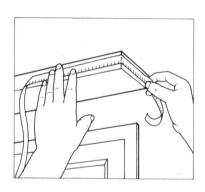

1 To estimate the amount of fabric required, measure the width as you would for curtains, allowing sufficient fabric for your chosen pleating style and for seams and hems (see page 25). Allow enough fabric to go round the sides. Depth should be in proportion to the curtains: generally speaking, you should allow 4cm (1½in) of valance for every 30.5cm (12in) of curtain length.

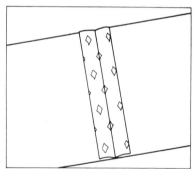

2 Cut out the pelmet and lining fabric, plus interlining or interfacing if you are using it. Join any widths where necessary as described on page 27, taking care to match any pattern repeats and remembering that, unlike curtains, a pelmet is unbroken across the total width of the window. A large design may have to be centred.

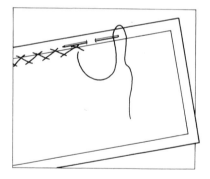

3 Make up the valance using the same technique as for a lined or interlined curtain. Turn in the two sides and along the bottom edge by 4cm (1½in), then tack and stitch. If using an interlining or stiffened interfacing, trim this to the size of the finished pelmet and herringbone stitch it into position between the side hems.

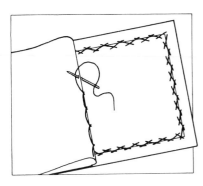

4 Lay the lining fabric over the interlining and lockstitch into position. To neaten, turn under the sides and bottom edge of the lining by around 2.5cm (1in) and slipstitch all round to hold in position. The pelmet is now ready for your chosen heading. This might be any of the curtain pleating effects, from simple to pinch pleats.

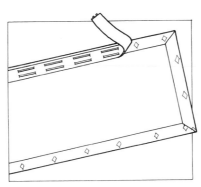

5 Pin and then tack the heading tape into position along the top of the wrong side of the valance, allowing around 3cm (1¼in) extra for turning over at the ends and loosening the cords before stitching, as detailed on page 35, steps 5 and 6. Machine stitch along all sides in the order described then knot and gather the cords.

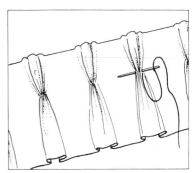

6 Whatever style of heading you have chosen for your pelmet, it is important when drawing up the gathers to make sure that the pleats are evenly distributed across the total width. If you are using one of the more sophisticated pleated heading effects, a couple of hand stitches in the base of each pleat gives a professional finish.

7 To hang a flounced fabric pelmet, attach curtain hooks to the back of the heading tape. These should be positioned about every 5cm (2in) for the valance to hang well. The hooks can be attached to a special rail in front of your curtain track, or be matched up to a series of eyelet rings screwed into a pelmet board.

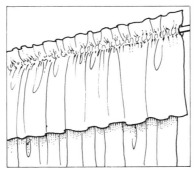

8 You can simplify the whole process by making a narrow casing along the top of the valance and threading it on to a metal pole or track fixed in front of the curtain rail. This does away with any kind of heading and produces a simple shirred effect rather than formal pleats, which may be better suited to the style of some rooms.

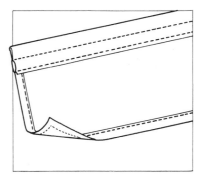

9 To make the casing, turn over a double hem of approximately 5cm (2in) at the top of the valance. Stitch this down with two rows of topstitching, the first 2.5cm (1in) from the top, and the second 2.5cm (1in) below that. These measurements can be adjusted to accommodate a larger rail or produce a more ruched heading.

shaped buckram pelmet

Where the valance pelmet produces a soft, flounced effect, a wooden pelmet board or stiffened fabric pelmet creates a far more formal and sophisticated tailored look. This might be better suited to decorative schemes which rely on crisp shapes and smart trims for their impact, rather than on a profusion of fabric frills and flounces. The wooden board is usually made from hardboard or plywood, and shaped like a narrow box or cut into contoured shapes such as scallops or crenellations. It may be painted to match your decorative scheme or covered in fabric to co-ordinate with the curtains. The alternative is a stiffened fabric pelmet, which creates a similar effect but can be removed for cleaning. This is attached to a plywood pelmet board, which looks like a shelf with end pieces, fixed above the window by means of angle irons. This should project by around 10cm (4in) to accommodate the track and curtains below. Covering the pelmet in fabric that matches the curtains makes the window look larger (see opposite).

Above: Decorative wooden pelmets like this one can be simply stained, varnished, painted or stencilled.

MATERIALS
BUCKRAM
FACING FABRIC TO MATCH OR
CO-ORDINATE WITH CURTAINS
INTERLINING
LINING FABRIC
MATCHING THREAD
PINS AND/OR TACKING THREAD
PAPER PATTERN
PELMET BOARD
HEADING TAPE
CURTAIN RINGS/VELCRO/TACKS

Unless you have given your curtains one of the grander pleated headings or are planning to fit a decorative pole, it is worth fitting some form of pelmet across the top of the window, both to hide the mechanics of curtain hanging and draping, and to make the window look more interesting.

If you are designing a traditional-style interior or if you live in a period property with rather grand windows, this more formal style of pelmet with its rigid form and often a shaped profile is particularly appropriate, especially where you do not want to use the more flounced, cottage-style valance pelmet. Traditional pelmets are often made from plywood, but you can now also buy ready-made plastic shapes which you cut to size and clip over your regular curtain track.

Many home furnishers prefer the option of cutting their own shapes in a stiffened fabric such as buckram. This is usually attached to a pelmet board by means of tacks, although rings and nails or Velcro enable the pelmet to be removed more easily for cleaning. If you do not relish the idea of making a template and cutting out a buckram shape, even this process can be simplified if you purchase a special self-adhesive stiffener with a peel-off backing paper. This is available ready-printed in a choice of pelmet styles, or on a grid if you prefer to devise your own. You simply cut out, cover with fabric and attach to the heading board.

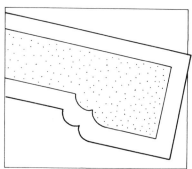

1 To make a stiffened fabric pelmet, estimate the fabric you require by measuring the pelmet board, including the side pieces, and adding 5cm (2in) for turnings. The depth of the pelmet will be influenced by the proportions of the curtains; as an approximate guide, allow 4cm (1½in) for every 30.5cm (12in) of curtain length, plus 10cm (4in) for the turnings.

2 If making a shaped pelmet, you will first need to draw up a paper pattern. Take a sheet of paper equal to the length of the board plus the sides, and fold it in half for symmetry. Draw on half the design you want, using a plate or a pair of compasses for scallops and curves, or a ruler and set square for square shapes and patterns.

3 Open out your finished pattern and pin it to the pelmet fabric: this will most likely be stiffened buckram. Cut out the shape carefully. Now, using the buckram as a guide, cut out the fabric that will be fixed to the front of the pelmet – usually chosen to match your curtains. Allow 10cm (4in) extra all round for turnings.

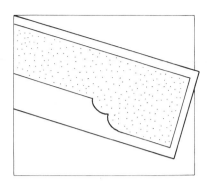

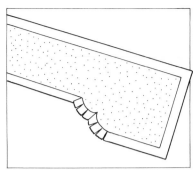

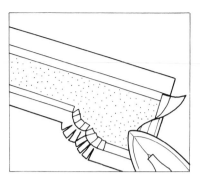

4 | If there is a distinctive pattern, it will look best if it can be centred; try to make any joins for extra fabric to the sides, matching the pattern repeat meticulously. Again using the buckram as a guide, cut out a piece of interlining, but this time 5cm (2in) larger all round. Interlining widths should be joined with a lapped seam.

5 | Lay the buckram exactly in the centre of the interlining, dampen the exposed edges slightly with a sponge or cloth and gradually fold over the buckram, a little at a time and pressing with a hot iron to encourage it to stick down. Snip any curves or corners with a sharp pair of scissors to encourage the material to lie flatter.

6 | Now lay your pelmet shape down in the centre of the main fabric, which should be wrong side uppermost. Dampen the buckram to help it stick, then fold up the edges of the decorative fabric as you did with the interlining, taking no more than 2.5cm (1in) at a time so that you can use the hot iron to press it down firmly.

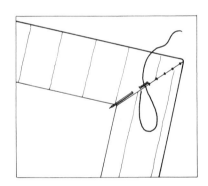

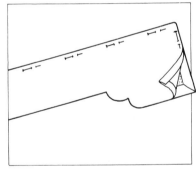

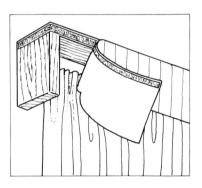

7 | Mitre the corners and slipstitch them into place for a neat finish. Slash the corners to remove any bulkiness, but reinforce with a few buttonhole stitches to prevent fraying. If you are planning to decorate the pelmet with some kind of trim or braid, stitch or glue it on to the right side of the pelmet at this stage.

8 | Taking the pelmet shape, use it to mark and cut a piece of curtain lining fabric, allowing 5cm (2in) extra all round. Turn over the seam allowance, trimming and slashing as necessary where the shape makes the fabric bulky, then pin this to the reverse of the pelmet, right side of the lining upper-most, and slipstitch into position.

9 | Pin simple heading tape along the top edge of the wrong side of the pelmet, turning in 1.5cm (½in) at the ends. Backstitch the ends and along the lower edge of the tape through to the buckram only. Handstitch curtain rings sufficient to hold the pelmet in place along the top edge and hang from small nails knocked into the pelmet board. Alternatively, tack directly on to the board, or use Velcro.

tracks and poles

The pole or track tucked away at the top of the window from which your curtains hang is not simply a necessary and functional object. It can affect the final look of the window quite considerably, and you need to give it serious consideration at the very earliest stages of planning your window. To start with, its height and length will influence the overall look and determine the amount of fabric you require. You will also need to choose a track or pole that is suited to the weight and style of fabric you have in mind. The curtain track shown opposite has been designed to be hidden by the curtain heading. You cannot cut costs without courting disaster: the simplest narrow track is only designed to hold the lightest-weight curtains, and will bow under the weight of a more elaborate effect. In fact, a sophisticated arrangement of curtains with separately hung linings, matching pelmet and blind will certainly demand a special track with extra hooks for the purpose.

Above: Traditional style curtain poles are available in a wide range of styles and finishes, both wooden and metal. They need to be chosen carefully to complement other furnishings.

TRACK OR POLE
FIXING BRACKETS
SCREWS AND WALLPLUGS
WOODEN BATTEN AND GLUE
(OPTIONAL)
PAINT/PAPER (OPTIONAL)

Curtain tracks and poles must be selected not just according to the type of curtains you are planning to hang and for how they will look, but also to fit the window correctly.

It is essential that your chosen rail or pole be long enough to clear the sides of the window frame; you may even prefer to take it well beyond the width of the window to let in maximum light. This is also a good visual device for making a window look larger than it really is. If the window is a difficult one without much room for fixing a track or rail, you will find solutions to these problems in the instructions on page 87. Another practical point that must be considered is whether the track or pole is strong enough for the job. Heavyweight fabrics, linings and interlinings will be too much for the simplest, narrowest styles and these will soon bow and can even break once the curtains are hung.

Unless you are planning to hide them behind a pelmet or valance, both tracks and poles can be decorated to fit in with your interior decorations. Some come ready finished: shiny metal tracks, poles in a mahogany, oak, modern or antiqued pine finish, or glossy brass complete with fancy finials. Plain plastic curtain tracks can be painted – maybe sponged, stippled or rolled – and if the runners attach to the back of the rail they can even be wallpapered. Wooden poles are also supplied unfinished for you to paint, stain or varnish as you choose.

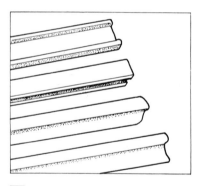

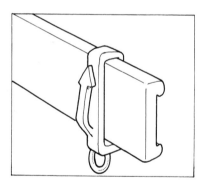

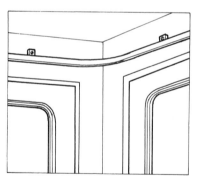

1 Your choice of track or pole will be determined by various practical and decorative factors. First decide where it is to be fitted, how long it needs to be and whether it will be hidden behind a pelmet, so need not be decorative. You can buy both wall- and ceiling-mounted fittings; some styles only come in a limited choice of lengths.

2 Modern rails tend to have an unobtrusive flat profile and incorporate hooks which ensure that the rail is covered by the curtains when drawn. Some can be painted or even wallpapered to match your decorative scheme without impeding the movement of the runners. They are generally made from aluminium or plastic with easy-glide nylon runners.

3 Most of the straight rails are designed to accept pull cords, so that the curtains can be pulled automatically from one side. If you have curved windows, such as a bay or bow window, you will need to buy a rail that can be bent round corners. Some of these can also be fitted with cords for drawing the curtains, so do check when buying.

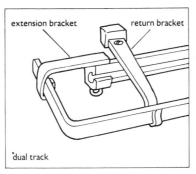

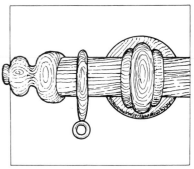

4 You can also purchase a variety of decorative poles which, while they do not offer such a sophisticated range of functions, can look splendid in the right setting and contribute much to the overall appearance of your window. These are available in various styles and sizes, from narrow brass poles to classical bronze-effect and timber finishes.

5 As well as the basic brackets essential for mounting tracks and poles, you can buy special types to suit particular situations. Extension brackets (*left, above*) hold the rail away from the wall; others accommodate a dual track. A return bracket (*right, above*) will enable the end of the rail to turn inwards; overlap arms allow one curtain to pass in front of another when they meet.

6 Most tracks come complete with brackets, and sometimes screws and wallplugs too. Poles are erected in much the same way, although some are only designed to have brackets at either end which makes them unsuitable for long windows. Rails are usually fitted to the wall above the window; drill holes to take the screws at regular intervals.

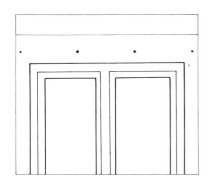

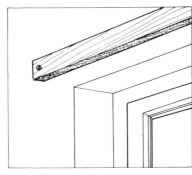

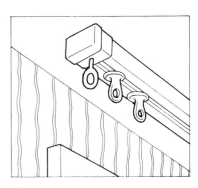

7 When marking the holes for the screws, use a spirit level to ensure that they are absolutely level. Do not use fewer brackets than the manufacturers recommend in an effort to save time, or the track may bend once the curtains are hung. Insert wallplugs and screw in the brackets using a screwdriver to make sure they are tightly fixed.

8 Sometimes the wall plaster is crumbly or there is a concrete lintel over the window which is too hard to drill into. Here a wooden batten made of 5 x 2.5cm (2 x 1in) timber is the solution. It should be longer than the lintel so that you can drill into brick and screw into it at either end. Glue the centre section and disguise the batten by painting or papering.

9 Where the window is close to the ceiling, fitting the rail to the ceiling may be the most practical option. Hollow wallplugs will not be strong enough, so you will have to find the position of the joists and screw into these using screws long enough to go right through the plaster. If the joists run the wrong way, fit battens between wall and joist.

CREATIVE VARIATIONS

The projects in this book will, hopefully, have been a source of both inspiration and practical guidance on a wide variety of very different but easy-to-achieve looks for your windows. But there are many more creative ways in which you can expand on these basic techniques to create original and eyecatching effects for your home.

DRAPED EFFECTS

It has become fashionable in recent years to do away altogether with curtain heading tapes and simply seam and hem the curtain widths before threading or draping the curtains over a pole. For a classical and completely 'no-sew' look, you can even take a long length of untouched fabric and wind it around the pole, allowing it to hang in natural folds to spill on to the floor at either side, at the same time creating a draped pelmet effect. Of course, the fabric cannot be drawn across the window at night, but as a stylish (and very speedy) form of dress curtain, perhaps used in conjunction with a blind or shutters, this can be very effective. Because the look is free-flowing and relaxed, with a suggestion of careless abundance, it is particularly suited to large amounts of inexpensive material such as undyed cotton, muslin or sheeting.

Another simple draped effect utilizes a short pole protruding from the top centre of the window, over which the fabric is thrown and held back at either side with cords or holdbacks. Or you could swathe the window in overlapping lengths of different-coloured net or dyed muslin; add interest to plain curtains with a fringed shawl wound around a pole to hang down at either side; or perhaps toss rush matting or a lightweight rug over a strong pole as a form of impromptu blind. Another idea would be to fasten a piece of quality fabric – nothing too flimsy and preferably lined – along the top and down one side of each window to fit the space exactly. Arrange things so that the lower unfixed corner of the fabric can be hooked up to the opposite side as required, and you have an ingenious and very stylish cross between blinds and curtains.

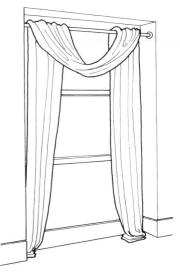

A simple cloth or length of fabric draped over a handsome pole can create an instant curtain.

Co-ordinated blind, curtains and pelmet create a splendid focal point.

Hook back fixed curtains for a 'sails' effect.

A single piece of decorative lace can make a fine screen.

MIX AND MATCH

If you really want to dress up a window, why not combine several effects together? Dress curtains are an obvious example for softening the sides of a window fitted with a roller or Austrian blind. These mock curtains have just enough drape in them to frame the window, but cannot be drawn. They can be as formal or informal as you choose, and be made from matching or contrasting fabric according to how dramatic an effect you wish to achieve. Where the window requires partial screening for privacy or as a protection from bright sunlight, net curtains or screens no longer have that old-fashioned, rather downmarket image, provided you use them stylishly. You can buy lace panels featuring traditional floral designs, spots, scallops, and even pictures of birds and animals that have a delightful period feel. Alternatively, for a more up-to-date look, dye plain nets in suitable pastel shades to suit your colour scheme. Some nets are frilled

Do not be afraid to experiment with different fabrics and effects. Here, blinds co-ordinate with a boldly bordered pelmet and dress curtains.

and ruched, but if this is too fussy for your taste, add your own decorations such as strips of lace, appliqué or embroidered detail. For a really stylish effect, buy softly patterned voiles to co-ordinate with your curtain fabric as an alternative to nets.

Other combination effects might make creative use of one or more of the fabric extras already mentioned such as tie-backs (page 72) or a valance pelmet (pages 76–79). Often the most effective (and least overpowering) option is not to choose an identical fabric to that of your curtains, but one that is more subtly co-ordinated with it. The design might be a smaller version of the main print, or feature spots and stripes instead of a floral, but in the same colours. You will find plenty of scope among today's co-ordinated fabric and paper ranges to inspire you; or, if you have a good eye for pattern and colour, you could put your own combinations together from different ranges.

An elaborate swagged pelmet creates a classical look.

TIE-BACKS AND PELMETS

Tie-backs might be little more than a simple strip of lined fabric hooked to the wall at either side and tied loosely around the curtain to keep it to one side. More elaborate types can be shaped and stiffened, given a contrasting edging or even a tasselled or embroidered trim in the Victorian style, and decorated with fabric bows, rosettes and flowers. For an instant effect, colour co-ordinated cord and matching tassels are available which make excellent tie-backs. Pelmets offer equally wide scope for being creative and highly decorative. The boxy style featured on page 80 is ideal for both formal and less fussy effects; a fabric flounce is naturally more frilly and feminine, but co-ordinates perfectly with other window features. This look can be emphasized further by actually using a shortened flounced blind as a deep pelmet. Alternatively, use several tie-backs, of varying lengths and employing scallops, tassels and draped fabric, for a rich, layered effect. If the unsewn draped look is a little too unstructured for your taste, develop the drapes into one of the most elaborate of pelmet effects – swags and tails. Here the fabric is scooped and draped across the centre of the window to fall in pointed tails (which can be as long or as short as you choose) on either side, and is usually arranged to show off a contrasting lining. Swags and tails often feature scrunched fabric rosettes to highlight each swoop of fabric.

ROLLER COASTING

The dressier blind effects, such as Austrian and Roman blinds, that use folds and gathers of fabric can be decorated with a contrasting border or perhaps lace, braid, buttons and bows, provided these are not likely to inhibit the folding or gathering action of the blind. But it is roller blinds that offer the greatest scope for highly individual and creative design if you have the inclination. That large, flat surface

Stencilling is a quick way to brighten up a plain roller blind.

provides all the opportunities of a blank canvas for painting, stencilling or decorating as your imagination and talents permit.

Stencils are easy to apply using fabric paints or crayons. You can buy them ready-cut in a wide choice of designs, including traditional florals, art deco style or modern geometrics. You could use these to apply not just a decorative border but a whole picture panel to the centre of the blind. Alternatively, trace off a favourite design, apply it to the blind and paint it in: if you need your chosen picture or pattern enlarged and are no good at freehand drawing, use a photocopier to blow up the design. This is an excellent way to personalize a blind for a children's room, as many of their favourite cartoon and nursery characters are easily copied and coloured in.

More ambitious perhaps is a complete *trompe-l'oeil* or picture blind. This would look good at the kitchen window, in the bathroom, or anywhere that has a rather dull view. Imagine gazing out at a tropical beach or distant hills instead of a brick wall and a row of dustbins! If you don't think your artistic talents are up to it, practise on a sheet of paper first – you might surprise yourself, and even the most impressionistic efforts can look quite realistic from a distance. One way to 'cheat' and achieve expert results is to pin or tape your fabric to the wall and to project a suitable view or picture on to it using a slide transparency and projector. You then simply paint over the image!

GLOSSARY

Appliqué: design cut from one fabric and stitched or glued to another.

Austrian blind: flounced-style blind made from gathered fabric.

Batten: long, narrow piece of timber.

Bay window: protruding window with its own roof and side walls rising from ground level.

Bias binding: strip of fabric cut across the bias and used for finished edges.

Bow window: a late-eighteenth- to early-nineteenth-century style of curved window.

Café curtain: a short, flat or gathered curtain covering the lower half of the window to provide privacy.

Cleat: wooden or metal device designed to secure rope or cord.

Dormer window: upper window with its own roof and sides, called cheeks, which protrude from the slope of a roof.

Finial: ornamental knob or similar end-piece used to decorate the end of a pole or post.

French windows: pair of narrow casement doors.

Grain: direction of weave and print of fabric.

Heading tape: corded tape stitched to the top of curtains and gathered to produce different pleated effects.

Mitring: neat finish for fabric corners.

Pelmet: valance, board or box at the head of the window.

Roller blind: flat panel of stiffened fabric fastened to a retractable roller mechanism.

Roman blind: style of window blind which gathers the fabric in flat, regular folds.

Ruched: frilled or gathered.

Screen: curtain blind, or sometimes used to describe a net curtain.

Selvedge: woven edge of a length of fabric.

Shades: curtain blinds.

Sill: wood, stone or concrete lip below the window which may be of any width depending on the thickness of the walls. Also called a window board.

Spirit level: instrument used to test the accuracy of a vertical or horizontal line.

Swag: generous sweep or drape of fabric.

Swatch: small sample or cutting of fabric.

Tack: baste two pieces of fabric together with long, loose stitches.

Tie-back: piece of fabric, cord or panel used to hold back a curtain from the window.

Topstitch: stitching on the right side of the fabric.

Track: metal or plastic rail used to suspend blinds and curtains.

Valance: narrow gather of fabric used to make a pelmet above the window and hide the curtain headings. Also used to describe a similar effect around the base of a bedcover.

ACKNOWLEDGEMENTS

Grateful thanks to Alex Ramsey, James Kerswell, Sue Walsh, Maggie Owen-Thomas and Ann Walsh for their invaluable assistance with photography for this book.

Photographs courtesy of:
Camera Press 52; Camera Press/IMS 4, 9, 32, 44, 57, 69, 72; Camera Press/Living 49; Choice catalogue: freephone 0800 269396 68, 85; Leanne from the Dorma Galleria Collection 77; Minoa from the Dorma Galleria Collection 76; Faber Blinds Ltd 56, 88; The Partners range from Forbo-Lancaster 33; Harrison Drape: 0121 766 6111 48; Houses & Interiors 13, 60; Alex Ramsay 40, 41, 53, 80, 81; Sanderson: 0171 584 3344 17; English Village Collection by Muriel Short 93; Zoo light resistant roller by Sunway Blinds 45; Masterpole from Swish 84; Mineralpole from Swish 61; Whiteheads Fabrics: 01903 212222/6 36, 64, 73; Michael Dunne/Elizabeth Whiting & Associates 37; Rodney Hyett/Elizabeth Whiting & Associates 65.

INDEX

Page numbers in *italic* refer to illustrations